THIS IS THE
HONEY

THIS IS THE HONEY

AN ANTHOLOGY OF CONTEMPORARY BLACK POETS

*Edited with an Introduction
by Kwame Alexander*

LITTLE, BROWN AND COMPANY
New York Boston London

For Jessie Redmon Fauset, Gwendolyn Brooks,
Dudley Randall, and Naomi Long Madgett,
champions of Black poets;
we remember you,
we say your name,
we give thanks.

Little, Brown and Company
Hachette Book Group
1290 Avenue of the Americas, New York, NY 10104
littlebrown.com

First Edition: January 2024

Little, Brown and Company is a division of Hachette Book Group, Inc. The Little, Brown name and logo are trademarks of Hachette Book Group, Inc.

The publisher is not responsible for websites (or their content) that are not owned by the publisher.

The Hachette Speakers Bureau provides a wide range of authors for speaking events. To find out more, go to hachettespeakersbureau.com or email hachettespeakers@hbgusa.com.

Little, Brown and Company books may be purchased in bulk for business, educational, or promotional use. For information, please contact your local bookseller or the Hachette Book Group Special Markets Department at special.markets@hbgusa.com.

ISBN 9780316417525
LCCN 2023941630

Permissions begin on page 363.

Printing 4, 2024

LSC-C

Printed in the United States of America

CONTENTS

THAT'S MY HEART RIGHT THERE

WHERE I'M FROM

DEVOTIONS

RACE RAISE RAGE: THE BLACKENED ALPHABET

WHEN I SEE THE STARS: PRAISE POEMS

INTRODUCTION

So much of the time, Black writers are expected to write about the woe. We are called to explore, explain, and expose those things and people and circumstances that make every attempt to arrest our community's development. And so we have, out of necessity, created a distinguished and affirming literature, from Phillis Wheatley to Maya Angelou to Mahogany Browne—who graciously offered the title to this anthology—in accordance with the actions of America. A poetry that revives. That resists. That fights back. As Amiri Baraka wrote in his 1979 poem "Black Art":

> *Poems are bullshit unless they are*
> *teeth or trees or lemons piled on a step...*
> *We want poems with fists...*
> *Let there be no love poems written*
> *until love can exist freely and*
> *cleanly...*

We also know, as Lucille Clifton reminded us, that *poems come out of wonder* too. That even though yesterday was filled with heartache, *we gon' be alright*. Because we are still here. And today is *gonna be a good day*. That is our testimony. Langston said it best:

Folks, I'm telling you,

birthing is hard

and dying is mean

so get yourself

a little loving

in between

This book is the *in between*. It's a gathering space for Black poets to
honor and celebrate. To be romantic and provocative. To be unburdened
and bodacious. The poetry in this collection is not us looking outward;
it's an unbridled selfie. To marvel at. And reflect. It's for us. But also it is
for you. The poems here are meant to inspirit, uplift, and rejoice. They
are unapologetically matter-of-fact Black. Poems full of hope and humor
and humanity of a proud people who hold the promise of tomorrow in
their hearts.

As a child, I was introduced to the Harlem Renaissance poets and
the Black Arts poets in my father's first editions of Woodie King's anthol-
ogies, *The Forerunners: Black Poets in America* and *Black Spirits: A Festi-
val of New Black Poets in America*. That was when I became enraptured
with poetry. Where I saw how clever and conscious wordplay could paint
a portrait of truth so divine and powerful, you felt reborn. In college, I
would discover Dudley Randall's *The Black Poets: A New Anthology* and
my professor Nikki Giovanni's *Night Comes Softly: An Anthology of Black
Female Voices*—which she self-published—and immediately feel the call
to arms as a poet with a responsibility to speak the truth to the people.
As a burgeoning writer and open-mic enthusiast in the 1990s engaging
with poets, from Washington, DC's It's Your Mug and 8 Rock Cultural
Center to Los Angeles' Leimert Park's World Stage to the Brooklyn

Moon Café, I carried around copies of Lindsay Patterson's *A Rock Against the Wind: African American Poems and Letters of Love and Passion* and E. Ethelbert Miller's *In Search of Color Everywhere: A Collection of African-American Poetry* and read and studied each piece, many by my peers, as if the books were a master class on *how to make a poet black, and bid him sing. This Is the Honey* continues the tradition of these elegant and essential primers. This is a bringing together of more than one hundred living voices — some emergent, some *Pulitzered*, some elders, ALL brilliant — superbly capturing the wonder of our story.

I am grateful to my dear friend the poet Marjory Wentworth for her keen and astute curatorial acumen in the field of African American poetry, and to Ndali Brume, Masie Ibrahim, and Elizabeth Quarles for their editorial assistance. This anthology comes exactly twenty-five years after I edited — with Kalamu ya Salaam — my first: *360 Degrees: A Revolution of Black Poets.* If that collection was a call to action, a response to the storm that felled us, this collection is the rainbow. Birds no longer caged. The sweet song of joy that comes from feeling free. Freer. Nikki said it best: *Poems are like clouds on a June morning or two scoops of chocolate ice cream on a sugar cone in August…* This is the honey indeed.

THE LANGUAGE
OF JOY

Quilting the Black-Eyed Pea
(We're Going to Mars)

Nikki Giovanni

We're going to Mars   for the same reason Marco Polo rocketed
                              to China
                    for the same reason Columbus trimmed
                        his sails on a dream of spices
                    for the very same reason Shackleton
                        was enchanted with penguins
                    for the reason we fall in love
It's the only adventure

We're going to Mars   because Perry couldn't go to the North
                              Pole without Matthew Henson
                    because Chicago couldn't be a city
                        without Jean Baptiste Du Sable
                    because George Washington Carver and
                        his peanut were the right partners for
                        Booker T.
It's a life seeking thing

We're going to Mars   because whatever is wrong with us will not
                        get right with us so we journey forth
                        carrying the same baggage
                        but every now and then leaving

one little bitty thing behind:

maybe drop torturing Hunchbacks here;

maybe drop lynching Billy Budd there;

maybe not whipping Uncle Tom to death;

maybe resisting global war.

One day looking for prejudice to slip........one day looking for
hatred to tumble by the wayside........one day maybe the
whole community will no longer be vested in who sleeps with
whom......maybe one day the Jewish community will be at
rest........the Christian community will be content....the
Muslim community will be at peace.......and all the rest of us
will get great meals at Holydays and learn new songs and sing
in harmony

We're going to Mars   because it gives us a reason to change

If Mars came here   it would be ugly

　　　　　　　Nations would ban together to hunt down

　　　　　　　　　and kill Martians

　　　　　　　and being the stupid and undeserving life

　　　　　　　　forms that we are

　　　　　　　we would also hunt down and kill

what would be termed

Martian Sympathizers

　　　　　As if the *Fugitive Slave Law* wasn't

　　　　　　bad enough then

　　　　　As if the so-called *War on Terrorism*

　　　　　　isn't pitiful Now

When do we learn and what does it take to teach us things

4

cannot be:

What we want

When we want

As we want

Other people have ideas and inputs

And why won't they leave Rap Brown alone

The future is ours to take

We're going to Mars   because we have the hardware to do it...

we have

Rockets and fuel and money and stuff

and the only

Reason NASA is holding back is they

don't know

If what they send out will be what they

get back

So let me slow this down;

Mars is 1 year of travel to get there......

plus 1 year of living on Mars.....

plus 1 year to return to Earth....

=3 years of Earthlings being in a tight space going to
an unknown place with an unsure welcome awaiting
them...tired muscles...unknown and unusual foods...harsh
conditions...and no known landmarks to keep them human...
only a hope and prayer that they will be shadowed beneath
a benign hand and there is no historical precedent for that
except this:

The trip to Mars can only be understood through Black Americans
I say, the trip to Mars can only be understood through Black Americans

The people who were captured and enslaved immediately
recognized the men who chained and whipped them and herded
them into ships so tightly packed there was no room to turn...
no privacy to respect...no tears to fall without landing on
another...were not kind and gentle and concerned for the state
of their souls...no...the men with whips and chains were
understood to be killers...feared to be cannibals...known
to be sexual predators...The captured knew they were in
trouble...in an unknown place...without communicable
abilities with a violent and capricious species...
But they could look out and still see signs of Home
        they could still smell the sweetness in the air
        they could see the clouds floating above the land they loved
But there reached a point where the captured could not only not
look back
        they had no idea which way "back" might be
        there was nothing in the middle of the deep blue water to
        indicate which way home might be and it was that
        moment...when a decision had to be made:
                Do they continue forward with a resolve to see
                this thing through or do they embrace the waters
                and find another world
In the belly of the ship a moan was heard...and someone
picked up the moan...and a song was raised...and that song
would offer comfort...and hope...and tell the story...

When we go to Mars........it's the same thing...it's Middle
   Passage
When the rocket red glares the astronauts will be able to see
themselves pull away from Earth...as the ship goes deeper
they will see a sparkle of blue...and then one day not only will
they not see Earth...they won't know which way to look...
and that is why NASA needs to call Black America

They need to ask us: How did you calm your fears...How
were you able to decide you were human when everything
said you were not...How did you find the comfort in the face
of the improbable to make the world you came to your world...
How was your soul able to look back and wonder

And we will tell them what to do: To successfully go to Mars
and back you will need a song...take some Billie Holiday for
the sad days and some Charlie Parker for the happy ones but
always keep at least one good Spiritual for comfort...You
will need a slice or two of meatloaf and if you can manage it
some fried chicken in a shoebox with nice moist lemon pound
cake...a bottle of beer because no one should go that far with-
out a beer and maybe a six-pack so that if there is life on Mars
you can share...Popcorn for the celebration when you land
while you wait on your land legs to kick in...and as you climb
down the ladder from your spaceship to the Martian surface...
look to your left...and there you'll see a smiling community
quilting a black-eyed pea...watching you descend

The Language of Joy

Jacqueline Allen Trimble

Black woman joy is like this:
Mama said one day long before I was born
she was walking down the street,
foxes around her neck, their little heads
smiling up at her and out at the world
and she was wearing this suit she had saved up
a month's paycheck for after it called to her so seductively
from the window of this boutique. And that suit
was wearing her, keeping all its promises
in all the right places. Indigo. Matching gloves.
Suede shoes dippity-do-dahed in blue.
With tassels! Honey gold. And, Lord, a hat
with plume de peacock, a conductor's baton that bounced
to hip rhythm. She looked so fine she thought
Louis Armstrong might pop up out of those movies
she saw as a child, wipe his forehead and sing
ba da be bop oh do de doe de doe doe.
And he did. Mama did not sing but she was skiddly-doing that day,
and the foxes grinned, and she grinned
and she was the star of her own Hollywood musical
here with Satchmo who had called Ella over and now they were all
singing and dancing like a free people up Dexter Avenue,
and don't think they didn't know they were walking in the footsteps
of slaves and over auction sites and past where old Wallace

had held onto segregation like a life raft, but this
was not that day. This day was for foxes and hip rhythm
and musical perfection and folks on the street joining in the celebration
of breath and holiness. And they did too. In color-coordinated ensembles,
they kicked and turned and grinned and shouted like church
or football game, whatever their religious preference. The air
vibrated with music, arms, legs, and years of unrequited
sunshine. Somebody did a flip up Dexter Avenue.
It must have been a Nicholas Brother in a featured performance,
and Mama was Miss-Lena-Horne-Dorothy-Dandridge
high-stepping up the real estate, ready for her close-up.
That's when Mama felt this little tickle. She thought
it might be pent-up joy, until a mouse squirmed out
from underneath that fine collar, over that fabulous fur,
jumped off her shoulder and ran down the street.
Left my mama standing there on Dexter Avenue in her blue
suit and dead foxes. And what did Mama do?
Everybody looking at her, robbed by embarrassment?
She said, "It be like that sometimes," then she and Satchmo,
Ella, and the whole crew jammed their way home.

Garden of the Gods

Ama Codjoe

The playbill is shut and I'm thinking
of the book Octavia Butler never wrote:
how it could begin with the death

of the last black man in the whole entire
world, which is the name of the play
we are about to see: "The Death of the Last

Black Man in the Whole Entire World
A.K.A. The Negro Book of the Dead."
My date and I share the armrest

and I'm staring at the black wisps
on his forearm picturing the hair no one
else can see: symmetrical except the patch

on his lower back. We stand to let three patrons
pass, press ourselves against the backs
of our seats. Sometimes when I kiss the man

beside me, I think of one of Butler's
protagonists who had the ability
to feel another's pleasure. I want to feel

what my lips taste like and how his *it feels*
good really feels. These days, real life
feels like science fiction and science fiction

can be truer than life—or at least
true to life, which is what this novel
would be: more real than local news,

a depiction (spoiler alert) of the fictions
of race and their real consequences.
And—there'd be a plot twist in the first

few pages: with his dying breath
the last black man in the whole entire world
would, like a god, animate a new one.

If Octavia Butler was alive to write it,
the rest of the novel would, in its entirety,
be about that. Mud oozing. The first forms

of life. The lights are dimming
and I see clearly what's beginning
to move. A large branch stretched

across most of the stage and a woman,
head-wrapped, gripping a watermelon
in her lap. Uncrossing and recrossing

my legs, I take one last look
at the arm beside me, dark and alive,
before another world pulls us away.

Labor

Jericho Brown

I spent what light Saturday sent sweating
And learned to cuss cutting grass for women
Kind enough to say they couldn't tell the damned
Difference between their mowed lawns
And their vacuumed carpets just before
Handing over a five-dollar bill rolled tighter
Than a joint and asking me in to change
A few lightbulbs. I called those women old
Because they wouldn't move out of a chair
Without my help or walk without a hand
At the base of their backs. I called them
Old, and they must have been; they're all dead
Now, dead and in the earth I once tended.
The loneliest people have the earth to love
And not one friend their own age — only
Mothers to baby them and big sisters to boss
Them around, women they want to please
And pray for the chance to say please to.
I don't do that kind of work anymore. My job
Is to look at the childhood I hated and say
I once had something to do with my hands.

Black Boys

Tony Medina

Black boys scrape their knees — they bleed
Black boys cry and scream — they tackle life like air
Gliding on wind — basking in a breeze

Black boys sit beneath trees — inhale fresh-cut grass
And dream
Black boys play with building blocks, are fascinated
By clocks — cradle skateboards under their arms

Black boys love basketball and books — toss footballs
And leaf through pages lost in stories and myths
Black boys love comic books and superheroes —
Are heroes to little sisters and brothers

Black boys love popcorn and watching movies
Love their grandmas and grandpas
Black boys hug and kiss their moms
And emulate their dads
Black boys wear their daddy's shoes and ties
Smear shaving cream on their smooth faces
Giggling in steamy mirrors

Black boys shine bright in sunlight
Build snowmen and have snowball fights

Black boys study the stars—looking
Through telescopes, lie on their backs
In tall grass, staring at the blanket of blue sky
At all the eyes smiling and twinkling
Down on them

Black boys like to hum and drum
Bebop hip hop—like to dance and sing
Jazz and scream

Black boys are three dimensions of beauty
Black boys go to church
Ride buses, go to school
Sit on stoops, fly kites, shoot hoops

Black boys like to sit in their quiet
And think about things

Black boys are made of flesh—
Not clay

Black boys have bones and blood
And feelings

Black boys have minds that thrive with ideas
Like bees around a hive
Black boys are alive with wonder and possibility
With hopes and dreams

Black boys be bouquets of tanka
Bunched up like flowers
They be paint blotched into a myriad of colors
Across the canvases of our hearts

We celebrate their preciousness and creativity
We cherish their lives

Navel

Robin Coste Lewis

We crawled out of her navel
one by one, then waited
until we were all here.

That lucid moment when
the last wet child learned to stand,
we began walking.

We walked slowly.
We took some time.
We took more than that.

When we began to grow
hungry, some offered to turn
themselves into animals.

Smiling, they said, Here, eat me.
Others turned into water, rivers, trees.
Some turned themselves to dirt

so we could walk a path. We crept
toward the edges, clawed and crawled to the top
of the world, and there we clung.

Instead of a mouth, a woman
spoke through a vibrant yellow
bill. Sometimes we visited the man
on the moon. Sometimes he let us
inside his house. Sometimes
his transparent hollow wife would dance.

Later, when people asked us,
Where did you come from?
We could only answer *water*.

A whole language comprised
of just one word. We walked
onto the water. We built houses

on the water. We had babies
on the water. We sewed clothes
made of water with needles made of ice.

The night so constant
changed us. The planets
taught us a vocabulary

without any alphabet.
The trees began to walk.
At night, the ocean glowed

green from underneath.

Our roofs were made of whale
ribs, our lamps were stone

that burned clear oil. And now
I've turned my face into this page
so we could sit here together again.

A Parable of Sorts

Malika Booker

We danced to rancorous tunes on spiked ground and
our knees sang with each puncture, so that several

agouti colonies, melanic in our russet strengths,
learned as wild rats to scurry or guard ourselves from

skin-spite. Immune from nocturnal drowsiness
we strong-bellied creatures assembled, campaigned;

gyrated to blowed trumpets and cradled songs, but,
us black rats with our rogue swagger that spoke

of foreign ports, pranced our survival shuffle in
night's murky dance halls. Each step our single

prayer, each jab our benediction. This tart sermon
containered our septic hurts and lean swaggers. On

the strike of dawn, we skittered from shadows, the
redeemed walking day's straight-road into warpland.

Boxing Lessons

LeRonn Brooks

I am a journeyman shadowboxing.

I am Quick Magic on the undercard.

I am lightning.

I am stitches

and I lead with a good hook;

and I have *such* a good hook.

I am a man leaning into a fight

with his chin taking questions:

What is the value of witnessing?

And what good does it do to fight at all?

But I am ready

and I am *so* ready.

I am a sucker-punch

and I am a flat-out brawl.

I am 36 cents in 2 games of dozens.

I have been half full

and I have been half-in.

I am an illegal traffic in pain

and I am the master of two hard palms.

I am a poetry of cheap shots.

I am quick footwork against the ropes.

I am the overhand right in good rum.

I am the speed-knot from the bum rush.

I am a standing 8 count on wobbly legs.

I am a kingdom of boxing hammers.

I am a gas-lit welterweight boxing smoke.

I am the drawl in cursive script.

I am the cheap shot in cheap flowers

and I am exactly what you mean by "low rent."

But I am ready

Oh, I am *so* ready

On Voting for Barack Obama with a Nat Turner T-Shirt On

Reginald Dwayne Betts

The ballot has never been a measure of forgiveness.
In prison, people don't even talk about voting,
about elections, not really, not the dudes
you remember, cause wasn't nobody Black
running no way. But your freedom hit just
in time to see this brother high-stepping with
the burden, with the albatross, willing
to confess that he knew people like you.
& you are free, you are what they call out
& off papers & living in a state where you
can cast a ballot. In prison, you listened
to ballot or the bullet & imagined that
neither was for you, having failed with
the pistol & expecting the ballot to be
denied. But nah, you found free & in line
notice that this is not like the first time
you & the woman you'd married got naked
& sweated & moaned & funked up a room
not belonging to either of you. That lady
is with you now & a kid is in your arms,
& you are wearing a Nat Turner T-shirt
as if to make a statement at the family
reunion. Everyone around you is Black,
which is a thing you notice. & you know

your first ballot will be cast for a man
who has the swag that seems inherited.
It's early but there is no crust in your eyes,
you wanted this moment like freedom.
You cast a ballot for a Black man in
America while holding a Black baby.
Name a dream more American than
that, especially with your three felonies
serving as beacons to alert anybody
of your reckless ambition. That woman
beside you is the kind of thing fools
don't even dream about in prison,
she lets you hold your boy while voting,
as if the voting makes you & him
more free. Sometimes, it's just luck.
Just having moved to the right state
after the cell doors stopped
clanking behind you. The son
in the arms of the man was mine,
& the arms of the man belonged
to me, & I wore a Nat Turner
T-shirt like a fucking flag, brown
against my brown skin.

After People Stop Asking About Me

Kyle Dargan

But everyone asks how is it to raise a daughter within

        this hissy fit christened *Trump's America*. My daughter's

breach into life: five months after that vote, that incision.

        She is eighteen-months-old now. Can count her own

way to sixteen. Knows maybe thirty animals. Orange

        or any other color remains as of yet un-coded

in her mind. She does not see any of *this*. Her world

        is chirping "bye-bye" to the bubbles in her bath

before she sleeps. Yes, it is harder than you might think

        to teach a being concepts you cannot recall

learning yourself. Repetition is useful, as is multisensory

        reinforcement. So raising my daughter in this moment,

that is what it feels like—finding so many ways to repeat

        one concept until it implants and she commands

a new pathway for communing with the world. It is work

        but it does not break me. In fact, I feel spared

the now until we are engaged in something innocent

        like a ride on the kiddie train through Wheaton

Regional Park. Not rearing, just cradling her legs in my lap—

        those instances when I regain my selfish

mind, its capacity to ponder how many years it might take

        to make an America in which my kiddo can count

on having fewer rights than her grandmother enjoyed,

or her great-grandmother who lived a life of dodging
dangerous men—even after she'd joined the police, kept a sidearm.
But who wants that escaping my mouth?
Instead I just point towards trees flanking the tiny tracks,
beckoning, "*Hoo's* that? Yes, baby. It's an owl."

Your Dream Is

Jason Reynolds

Your dream is the mole
behind your ear,
that chip in your
front tooth,
your freckles.

It's the thing that makes
you special,
but not the thing that makes
you great.

The courage in trying,
the passion in living,
and the acknowledgement
and appreciation of
the beauty happening around
you does that.

A New Day Dawns

Nikky Finney

On the occasion of the Confederate flag falling in South Carolina,
July 10, 2015

It is the pearl-blue peep of day.
All night the palmetto sky
Was seized with the aurora
And alchemy of the remarkable.
A blazing canopy of newly minted
Light fluttered in while we slept.
We are not free to go on as if
Nothing happened yesterday.
Not free to cheer as if all our
Prayers have finally been answered
Today. We are free only to search
The yonder of each other's faces,
As we pass by, tip our hat, hold a
Door ajar, asking silently,
Who are we now? Blood spilled
In battle is two-headed: horror &
Sweet revelation. Let us put the
Cannons of our eyes away forever.
Our one and only Civil War is done.
Let us tilt, rotate, strut on. If we,
The living, do not give our future

The same honor as the sacred dead
Of then and now—we lose everything.
The gardenia air feels lighter on this
New day, guided now by iridescent
Fireflies, those atom-like creatures
Of our hot summer nights, now begging
Us to team up and search with them
For that which brightens every
Darkness. It will be just us
Again, alone, beneath the swirling
Indigo sky of South Carolina. Alone &
Working on the answer to our great
Day's question: *Who are we now?*
What new human cosmos can be made
Of this tempest of tears, this upland
Of inconsolable jubilation? In all our
Lifetimes, finally, this towering
Undulating moment is here.

Carolina Prayer

Justin Phillip Reed

Let the blood if your belly must have it, but let it
not be of me and mine. Let my momma sleep.
Let her pray. Let them eat. Let the reverend's
devil pass over me. Let the odds at least
acknowledge us. Let the breasts be intact,
the insulin faithfully not far, and let the deep
red pinpoint puddle its urgency on a pricked
fingertip. Let the nurse find the vein the first time.

Let the kerosene flow and let my grandma praise
her bedside lord for letting her miss another winter.
Let me be just a little bit bitter so I remember:
Your columns and borders aint but the fractured,
the broke clean, the brownest gouges in the blades
of our great-great-great-shoulders. Let me leave
and come back when my chest opens for you wider
than your ditches did to engorge my placeless body.

The mosquito-thick breath in your throat coats my skin
and it almost feels as if you love me. Let the AC
drown out the TV. Let the lotion bottle keep a secret
corner til Friday. Let Ike, Wan, D-Block, all my brother's
brothers ride through the weekend. Let the cop car
swerve its nose into night and not see none of them.

Let us smell rain. Let the breeze through an oak hymn
the promise that keeps us waking. Let the cicada
unwind while hushpuppy steam slips out the knot
of a tourist's hand, and let him hear in it legends
of how hot grease kept the hounds and the lash at bay.

Inescapable Country

Mark McMorris

Inside the world, the world is present.
It fills the mind with whistling
of birds, the golden flowers of pouis.

The ravines, along which scouts
pressed their enemies to a standstill,
throw up white blossoms of azaleas.

The paths are steep to the villages
splashed on the blue mountain ridges.
The cows in the pasture barely stir.

Something about pastoral calms
the violent heart, wherein desire
takes form in the visible world

Bending a corner, you see it green
as it once was and will be then
and always with the mind's deceit.

Blood Memory

Ronda Taylor

A

drop

in time

back when

fervent hands

praised 'til sweat

like drops of blood shed

on soil we tread. With clipped

wings, voices sing of freedom carried

through the air we breathe. This love is

a revolution, abiding in the vine of our blood-

line. We are the blood bought heirloom stained

redemption red. Our bodies house pain aching to

not be forsaken, yet joy abounds like a balm that

will prevail. Across the endless sky, we are stars

burning bright that cannot be extinguished.

Hope flows like fire shut up in our bones,

we dance like a flame cause it ain't

nothing but the

Blood.

The Nightflies

Sheree Renée Thomas

I remember the place
where nightflies sing like stars
their gilded wings reflect
the dark moon's glide
metallic shimmer, rhythmic hum
beat out a windblown pattern
foretell melodic monsoons
and electric rain showers

Always they came in the monsoon nights
the clouds angry and invisible
in the luminous sky, the submerged fields
lit by black lightning, its lingering
sulphuric smell a pheromone
the air heavy with the scent of storms
that do not break
the skies grown dense, exhale anticipation

And suddenly the night air
would be gauze wings, silent
inevitable as desire
how the light
caught the dark gleam of bodies
pale arcs plunging to fire

that brief gossamer blaze
like hearts that love only when burned

Mornings after the storm
my sisters would sweep out
piles of pale wings,
torn and shimmerless...

I remember the wet trembling
when we were like nightflies
blind bodies crawling
antlike in desperate circles
flung out in deep space
searching for the flame

Healing

Lolita Stewart-White

Night has brought this offering
Scent of his whiskey skin
   Dear Diaspora:
   I am black balm soothing
   I am black balm soothing
   I am black balm soothing
   A smoke prayer
Burn of amen in our throats
Bloodline dope like kinfolk passed down
Thick of our loveliness
We are the ones we've been waiting for
My lover unfurls his Union Blue
I turn the cool side of my finger north

This Is the Honey

Mahogany L. Browne

There is no room on this planet for anything less than a miracle
We gather here today to revel in the rebellion of a silent tongue
Every day, we lean forward into the light of our brightest designs
    & cherish the sun
Praise our hands & throats
      each incantation, a jubilee of a people dreaming wildly
Despite the dirt
beneath our feet
or the wind
pushing against
our greatest efforts

Soil creates things
Art births change
This is the honey
    & doesn't it taste like a promise?
Where your heart is an accordion
    & our laughter is a soundtrack

Friend, dance to this good song—
look how it holds our names!

Each bone of our flesh-homes sings welcome

O look at the Gods dancing

    as the rain reigns against a steely skyline

Where grandparents sit on the porch & nod at the spectacle

in awe of the perfection of their grandchildren's faces

Each small discovery unearthed in its own outpour

Tomorrow our daughters will travel the world with each poem

    & our sons will design cities against the backdrops of living

museums

    Yes! Our children will spin chalk until each equation bursts a

familial tree

Rooted in miraculous possibilities

& alive

THAT'S MY HEART RIGHT THERE

This Is an Incomprehensive List of All the Reasons I Know I Married the Right Person

Clint Smith

Because on weekends you wrap your hair with a scarf
and you have so many different scarves that come in
so many different colors and now when I'm out in the world
every time I see a colorful scarf I think of you and I think
of the weekends which are the best days because they are
the days that you and I don't have to worry about work
or deadlines just bagels and bacon and watching this small
human we've created discover the world for the first time.
Because when you laugh you kind of cackle, no I mean you
really cackle like you take a deep breath in and out comes
something unfiltered and unrehearsed and it's cute
but also scary and isn't that the perfect description of love?
Because when you watch *The Voice* you talk to the judges
as if they are waiting for your consultation. Because you
always ask the restaurant to make your pizza extra crispy
and then you put it in the oven for another thirty minutes
anyway after they deliver it. Because when you wake our son
up in the morning you are always singing. Because when
I read you poems I love you always close your eyes
and tell me your favorite line. Because on my birthday
you had my friends make barbecue and we had leftovers
for weeks. Because I like my cinnamon rolls

with maple syrup and honey mustard and you still kiss me

in the morning. Because you hold my hand

when I'm scared and don't know how to say it.

That's My Heart Right There

Willie Perdomo

We used to say,
That's my heart right there.

As if to say,
Don't mess with her right there.

As if, don't even play,
That's a part of me right there.

In other words, okay okay,
That's the start of me right there.

As if, come that day,
That's the end of me right there.

As if, push come to shove,
I would fend for her right there.

As if, come what may,
I would lie for her right there.

As if, come love to pay,
I would die for that right there.

Refractions

You're mowing the lawn — the percussive hiccup
of hip-hop in your earbuds when Black Thought spits:

Some nights I lay awake and feel all of my thoughts runnin' I tally my
regrets, upsets, and shortcomings...
And the squeals cut through the drums. It's your daughters —
Jade Rose chasing her big sis, yelling "Jazmyn"
as they dash around the birdbath,

your wife smiling at their bright joy
as she plants her begonias and blue hostas.

It's spring. 80 degrees.
Nearly hot enough to warp your view of distant things.

And didn't this life once seem an illusion — the future a liquid tease,
stunningly bent like colorful refractions?

You were once light, bouncing between love's missed opportunities
those decades ago,

when you and the guys
crowded a traffic light control box you all made your table,

nearly oblivious to passersby except the sistas blossoming in their
sundresses,

the ones who tensed up as they got close, having to pass y'all on their
way
to drinks and Happy Hour Specials, waiting for catcalls
that didn't come.

And when there were no thirsty stares,
did they see brothas aching for love's prism
to send each of them beaming in all directions?
Yo, D said, *I want a family.*
J shook his head, *This single life is for the birds.*

Is that why the sistas lingered, just close enough to hear y'all doo
wapping blues on a Friday with the late spring light dawdling beyond
the threshold of dusk?

Is this why one of them found the courage to approach and said, *I never
knew guys talked about things like this?*

Hadn't you popped your bulb at what looked promising before she
flicked you away like a cigarette
from a driver-side window? Hadn't you done the same?
And a world away, your wife had her own thorny journey.

Regrets are stones along a path everyone travels
before they're enlightened.

Yours brought you here

to a house on a sunny corner, your wife watering the bushes.

You take in the humid air spiced by your daughters' laughter splitting
    this life

into its splendid bright angles.

I wish my love was here

Kurtis Lamkin

I wish my love was here
She would know what to do with such a day
She would wipe the sun and sea from her shoulders
And rub them deep into my palms, and
When the salt and sand was gone
She would kiss my hands and say "there...."
I wish she was here

I know she is in me
Even amid the crashing and foaming around me,
Her tenderest sigh.
I'm not alone
But I miss her. I miss her so much. And I don't know what to do.
She would know, my love, if she was here.

tripping
kwansaba

Van G. Garrett

one time i drove across the country
to see a woman i met once
and knew well in letters and photos
before sleek fancy phones and fast tools
when postage stamps were not a quarter
and a tank of gas took you
to the light arms of your dreams

Fruitful

Evie Shockley

you grow my garden. no, you are
        the whole of it: the beds of zinnias,
   tiger lilies, begonias, petunias, in all
          their taken-for-granted variety :: irises

waving purple flags from the tops
        of long stalks :: daffodils and violets by
   the bushel, rhododendrons and azaleas
        by the bush. you are the greenhouse

in the western quadrant, the rainforest
        inside, and the delicate herd of orchids,
   strange by stranger, each out-thriving
        the other. not just lovely, you're

the courtyard, central, complete
        with benches for contemplating
   the round, still pool, an eye gazing
        back at the ones looking down. you're

the meadow of tall grasses that hide
        everything but the sound of the stream ::
   the arched boughs of the peach orchard,
        the rows of beans, corn, greens, gourds,

the root vegetables, the parsley, sage,

        rosemary, and chives, oregano, basil,

   and, yes, all the thyme in the world.

         you're the stand of aspens waving me

on :: the grove of willows that arc

       and cascade, but never weep :: the oaks,

    maples, and birches encircling the verge.

        here, i become my best self, i exist at

peace with birds and bees, no knowledge

      is denied me: i eat the apple, speak

   with the snake, and nothing as obnoxious

        as an angel could oust me from this soil,

the plot where the best of my stories

     has its genesis, and finds its end.

Poem That Begins w/a Tweet About Gwendolyn Brooks

Mitchell L. H. Douglas

Gwendolyn Brooks was a Jeopardy! question no one could answer tonight.
That's a metaphor too painful to wrap my head around.

& I said, "The poem is about Love
because all poems are about Love,"

& you rolled your eyes so hard
I thought they would snap back to center

w/cherries & diamonds. The flit
of your lashes renders me nameless & I fall

blank for what feels like a block. Falling
is a metaphor for my life: unsettled,

unmoored. I capitalize Love
because it is bigger than what we are

or what we give credit for: oaken,
open. For that, you have no answer,

your breath in kitchenettes:
hal/ved, qu/art/er/ed — cut again.

Love Poem

Cameron Awkward-Rich

Dear woman, listening with your mouth
pursed into a false ear, which cannot—

despite the clarity with which my sisters,
who are poets & so precise

as an incision, describe how they are called
out of their blood into the same work—

get over how both women tower
gracefully & both, of course, are black

so become, in your mouth, mother
& child, had to share a body

been the same person. I suppose I'm grateful
when I can leave myself for long enough

to let a stranger or a love inside me, to be held
open as a tunnel for all the midnight traffic

or only you, whose face is not my face
until it is by some dark magic & oh, boy.

Dear dear boi. Whose body I slip into,
wear as a jacket against the rain.

May Perpetual Light Shine

Patricia Spears Jones

We have encountered storms
Perfect in their drench and wreck

Each of us bears an ornament of grief
A ring, a notebook, a ticket torn, scar
It is how humans know their kind—

What is known as love, what can become
the heart's food stored away for some future
Famine

Love remains a jewel in the hand, guarded
Shared fragments of earth & air drift & despair.

We ponder what patterns matter other than moons and tides:
musical beats—rumba or waltz or *cha cha cha*
cosmic waves like batons furiously twirling
colors proclaiming sparkle of darkness
as those we love begin to delight
in the stars embracing

Forcing it

Antoinette Brim-Bell

When the magnolia trees began dropping
their flowers out of season, I knew
it was time to let you go, but
old folks say, shock a branch — make
it bloom, with plastic wrap
water in a jar,
a little light
enough time —
some space —
wait.

In My Rush

Jonterri Gadson

The first time I saw myself
reflected in well-water,

I became light. Now no one knows
how to hold me. A valley is nothing

but the lowest point in the curve
of a woman's hip; a river — nothing —

if not her sway. Lightbearer translates
to Lucifer. I still want to be held. Hold me

like sound — in your throat,
with your breath, on your tongue.

I'll be a river on purpose.
We'll make a braid of our legs

Characteristics of Life

Camille T. Dungy

A fifth of animals without backbones could be at risk
of extinction, say scientists.
—*BBC Nature News*

Ask me if I speak for the snail and I will tell you
I speak for the snail.
                  I speak of underneathedness
and the welcome of mosses,
                        of life that springs up,
little lives that pull back and wait for a moment.

I speak for the damselfly, water skeet, mollusk,
the caterpillar, the beetle, the spider, the ant.
                       I speak
from the time before spinelessness was frowned upon.

Ask me if I speak for the moon jelly. I will tell you
             one thing today and another tomorrow
   and I will be as consistent as anything alive
on this earth.

             I move as the currents move, with the breezes.
What part of your nature drives you? You, in your cubicle
ought to understand me. I filter and filter and filter all day.

Ask me if I speak for the nautilus and I will be silent
as the nautilus shell on a shelf. I can be beautiful
and useless if that's all you know to ask of me.

Ask me what I know of longing and I will speak of distances
between meadows of night-blooming flowers.
I will speak
the impossible hope of the firefly.

You with the candle
burning and only one chair at your table must understand
such wordless desire.

To say it is mindless is missing the point.

As Serious as a Heart Attack

Kalamu ya Salaam

i have never been fully domesticated
but i have been civilized

by women taught that the heart
is more than a muscle

a life drum whose function is
both physical blood pumping
and spiritual longing to be embraced

but love, ah love is a river
we may get wet
but we can never drink it all
love always flows on
more than we can ever swallow

no matter how thirsty
we claim to be

The Talk

Gayle Danley

Pretty soon we'll have the talk.

She'll ask me where babies come from

And I will lie to her:

"Babies come from the chance meeting of sperm and egg

See the man deposits his sssperm which is like a pudding

into the woman's vvagina and it travels up this tube-y thing

and only one of them gets the prize and bing! A cell becomes

a fetus becomes baby becomes you.

Go do your homework."

She will wait for me to calm down,

her eyes patient requiring the truth

and I will tell her:

"Babies come from Friday nights melted into Saturday mornings;

the Isley Brothers and 3 or 4 glasses of white zin; miniskirts

and aching zippers; sofa cushions sweaty and OGODTHECONDOMBROKE;

Babies come from blue lights and e.p.t. tests and the wet spot on clean

sheets;

Lonely knees that bump beneath the table; love letters sealed

with a miss and $758 phone bills; eyeliner and lips to match; muscled

Thighs and a sweet, milky quarter of yes in the center of pink panties.

You came from this: a separated daddy and a desperate mama;

A ripped sonogram and hours spent on hardwood floors asking

girlfriends:

Should I go through with this?

Grandma's washboard and the dust tracks Grandaddy made when he
left her with five girls to maim

You came from this: Maryland rain, nights of shag carpet lovin' and
days
Just $2 short of the rent;
And one afternoon you came
I wanted your father so badly it hurt
Even took his last name and flung it behind yours like a spare tire
Whatever he gave me was never enough
It was like his love was a sieve
And my desire for him
Water
I was insane
Packed my dreams in a U-Haul and moved them to MD
Nothing better to do
30 and scared
You came from this:
Collision of longing
Tongue kissing and shame
The emptiness at the corner of GA Avenue
And the fullness of swollen ankles and readjusted dreams
You came from:
A poet and a singer
Fists and car keys
Peach cobbler and gumbo
Love
And that last dirty fight on the Beltway

You came baby
You came, here"

And she'll say:
"Mama, babies come from peach cobbler?"
and I'll say
yes.

Crows in a Strong Wind

Cornelius Eady

Off go the crows from the roof.
The crows can't hold on.
They might as well
Be perched on an oil slick.

Such an awkward dance,
These gentlemen
In their spottled-black coats.
Such a tipsy dance,

As if they didn't know where they were.
Such a humorous dance,
As they try to set things right,
As the wind reduces them.

Such a sorrowful dance.
How embarrassing is love
When it goes wrong

In front of everyone.

How We Made You

Kwame Alexander

In the future
when you're newly married
and the two of you
are half hanging off your bed
fingers playing in each other's locks
your legs braided
loud garbage trucks beeping outdoors
no whining children yet to cook for
and you're talking about leaving your job
or whose family to visit for Christmas
or how lucky you are to be loved like this
or whatever it is you talk about
after making love in the early morning
I want you to know
that before our uncoupling
your mother and I used to work the door
at a jazz club in Washington, DC,
and every Thursday night we'd stand at the entrance
collecting covers
greeting friends and regulars
feeding each other jerk wings
kissing the hot sauce from our lips
joking and laughing about this and that
holding each other when it got chilly

and later when we'd get back to our one-room apartment

on the other side of the bridge

we'd spread the money out on the bed

count our haul

smile if we could pay the rent

worry if we couldn't

and then we'd make our own music

and without fail

the woman next door would bang on the walls

and tell us to turn it down

but we wouldn't

because we couldn't

because we knew how lucky we were

to be loved like that.

Weathering Out

Rita Dove

She liked mornings the best—Thomas gone
to look for work, her coffee flushed with milk,

outside autumn trees blowsy and dripping.
Past the seventh month she couldn't see her feet

so she floated from room to room, houseshoes flapping,
navigating corners in wonder. When she leaned

against a doorjamb to yawn, she disappeared entirely.

Last week they had taken a bus at dawn
to the new airdock. The hangar slid open in segments

and the zeppelin nosed forward in its silver envelope.
The men walked it out gingerly, like a poodle,

then tied it to a mast and went back inside.
Beulah felt just that large and placid, a lake;

she glistened from cocoa butter smoothed in
when Thomas returned every evening nearly

in tears. He'd lean an ear on her belly

and say: *Little fellow's really talking,*

though to her it was more the *pok-pok-pok*
of a fingernail tapping a thick cream lampshade.

Sometimes during the night she woke and found him
asleep there and the child sleeping, too.

The coffee was good but too little. Outside
everything shivered in tinfoil—only the clover

between the cobblestones hung stubbornly on,
green as an afterthought....

Want Could Kill Me

Xan Forest Phillips

I know this

from looking

                into store fronts

                taste buds voguing
alight from the way

treasure glows

                when I imagine

                pressing its opulence
into your hand

I want to buy you

                a cobalt velvet couch

                all your haters' teeth
strung up like pearls

a cannabis vineyard

                and plane tickets

to every island

on earth

but my pockets

are filled with

lint and love alone
touch these inanimate gods

to my eyelids

when you kiss me

linen leather

gator skin silk

satin lace onyx

marble gold ferns

leopard crystal
sandalwood mink

pearl stiletto

matte nails and plush

lips glossed
in my 90s baby saliva

pour the glitter

over my bare skin

                    I want a lavish life
us in the crook

of a hammock
                    incensed by romance

                    the bowerbird will
forgo rest and meals

so he may prim
                    and anticipate amenity

                    for his singing lover
call me a gaunt bird

a keeper of altars
                    shrines to the tactile

                    how they shine for you
fold your wings

around my shoulders
                    promise me that

                    should I drown
in want-made waste

the dress I sink in
                    will be exquisite

When Macnolia Greases My Hair

A. Van Jordan

Every drop of coconut oil
Is a kiss on my scalp;
Every twist of black strands,
An embrace; every groove parted
By her comb, a drawn curtain
Through which I invite her to walk;
Every struggle to untangle my coils,
A trill in a song from her voice;
And when the songs won't come.
We wrap our skins in silence,
And when the silence gets too loud,
We wrap ourselves in each other.

"[love letter to self]

Warsan Shire

i don't think so. but, i forgive you, girl, who tallied stretch marks into reasons why no one should get close. i forgive you, silly girl, sweet breath, decent by default. i forgive you for being afraid. did everything betray you? even the rain you love so much made rust out of your jewellery? i forgive you, soft spoken girl speaking with fake brash voice, fooling no one. i see you, tender even on your hardest days. i forgive you, waiting for him to call, i forgive you, the diets and the cruel friends. especially for that one time you said 'i fucking give up on love, it's not worth it, i'd rather be alone forever'. you were just pretending, weren't you? i know you didn't mean that. your body, your mouth, your heart, made specifically for loving. sometimes the things we love, will kill us, but weren't we dying anyway? i forgive you for being something that will eventually die. perishable goods, fading out slowly, little human, i wouldn't want to be in a world where you don't exist."

a poem about you and me and the new country

Anis Mojgani

Oh, the glorious fightings I would start for you

I wish to hold you in this bed forever
the blue wilderness on your tongue
the country of your arms
this is my body worshipping

a new country of light
stamping our passports as we pass

what a sound my spirit makes
when I am not looking
like a zipper opening up an ocean
the Eiffel tower bending towards the earth to tell it a secret

pushing a flute
out of the bone of your lips is a mystery
what mountain birthed your heart

you are such magnificent poems

I want to rub my face all over you

later when standing in the kitchen

breaking the eggs for you
you call out
and say what a lovely sound

Patience

Ross Gay

Call it sloth; call it sleaze;
call it bummery if you please;
I'll call it patience;
I'll call it joy, this,
my supine congress
with the newly yawning grass
and beetles chittering
in their offices
beneath me, as I
nearly drifting to dream
admire this so-called weed which,
if I guarded with teeth bared
my garden of all alien breeds,
if I was all knife and axe
and made a life of hacking
would not have burst gorgeous forth and beckoning
these sort of phallic spires
ringleted by these sort of vaginal blooms
which the new bees, being bees, heed;
and yes, it is spring, if you can't tell
from the words my mind makes
of the world, and everything
makes me mildly or more
hungry—the worm turning

in the leaf mold; the pear blooms

howling forth their pungence

like a choir of wet-dreamed boys

hiking up their skirts; even

the neighbor cat's shimmy

through the grin in the fence,

and the way this bee

before me after whispering

in my ear dips her head

into those dainty lips

not exactly like one entering a chapel

and friends

as if that wasn't enough

blooms forth with her forehead dusted gold

like she has been licked

and so blessed

by the kind of God

to whom this poem is prayer.

Figurative Language

A$iahMae

My mama doesn't speak of love

We feel it in the full dinners before the graveyard shifts

And the crisp pleats in our "good" clothes

She greases love on my scalp and my edges

Shuffles love by robbing Peter to pay Paul

Love be her ASL on good days.

Mama doesn't speak of love

So we find a bridge in Mary J. Blige records

Mary be Mama's Valentine's Day

Mama's girl's night

Mama's anniversary

Mary morphs mama's vocal chords and

we feel love dancing on the freshly vacuumed carpet in the hallway

Bouncing off walls next to family photos and magazine pages

Playing tetherball with sun beams

Love done started a concert in the kitchen.

Love done wrapped herself around us

Smelling like warm, creamed grits

and Black Woman incenses

Skin the color of them pancakes she just flipped

With the edges perfectly crisp

With her edges perfectly laid

Love got her scarf still intact

And her silk robe to match

Running on 4 hours of sleep

Anticipating that extra shift she picked up

So I could go on the class trip

Love sits my plate in front of me

With a forehead kiss

And a song about heartbreak falling from her lips

And I know what love is

Without ever uttering her name

Because I know her face

And her voice

And when she sings to me

I never have to wonder.

I always ask for an encore.

I always know she's prepared.

hello

Sean Hill

She, being the midwife
and your mother's
longtime friend, said
I see a heart; can you
see it? And on the grey
display of the ultrasound
there you were as you were,
our *nugget,* in that moment
becoming a shrimp
or a comma punctuating
the whole of my life, separating
its parts—before and after—,
a shrimp in the sea
of your mother, and I couldn't
help but see the fast
beating of your heart
translated on that screen
and think and say to her,
to the room, to your mother,
to myself *It looks like*
a twinkling star.
I imagine I'm not
the first to say that either.
Unlike the first moments

of my every day,

the new of seeing you was *the* first

—deserving of the definite article—

moment I saw a star

at once so small and so

big, so close and getting closer

every day, I pray.

Delores Jepps

Tim Seibles

It seems insane now, but
she'd be standing soaked
in schoolday morning light,
her loose-leaf notebook
flickering at the bus stop,
and we almost trembled

at the thought of her mouth
filled for a moment with both
of our short names. I don't know
what we saw when we saw
her face, but at fifteen there's
so much left to believe in,

that a girl with sunset
in her eyes, with a kind smile,
and a bright blue miniskirt softly
shading her bare thighs   really
could be *The Goddess.* Even
the gloss on her lips sighed
Kiss me   and you'll never

do homework again. Some Saturdays
my ace, Terry, would say, "Guess

who was buying Teaberry gum
in the drugstore on Stenton?"
And I could see the sweet
epiphany still stunning his eyes

and I knew that he knew
that I knew he knew   I knew—
especially once summer had come,
and the sun stayed up till we had
nothing else to do but wish
and wonder about *fine sistas*

in flimsy culottes and those *hotpants!*
James Brown screamed about: Crystal
Berry, Diane Ramsey, Kim Graves,
and *her.* This was around 1970: Vietnam
to the left of us, Black Muslims
to the right, big afros all over my

Philadelphia. We had no idea
where we were, how much history
had come before us—how much
cruelty, how much more dying
was on the way. For me and Terry,
it was a time when everything said

maybe, and maybe being blinded
by the beauty of a tenth grader

was proof that, for a little while,
we were safe from the teeth
that keep chewing up the world.
I'd like to commend

my parents   for keeping calm,
for not quitting their jobs or grabbing
guns   and for never letting up
about the amazing "so many doors
open to good students." I wish

I had kissed
Delores Jepps. I wish I could
have some small memory of her
warm and spicy mouth to wrap
these hungry words around. I

would like to have danced with her,
to have slow-cooked to a slow song
in her sleek, toffee arms: her body
balanced between the Temptations'
five voices and me—a boy anointed

with puberty, a kid with a B
average and a cool best friend.
I don't think I've ever understood
how lonely I am, but I was

closer to it at fifteen because
I didn't know anything: my heart
so near the surface of my skin

I could have moved it with my hand.

The Ear Is an Organ Made for Love

E. Ethelbert Miller

(for Me-K)

It was the language that left us first.
The Great Migration of words. When people
spoke they punched each other in the mouth.
There was no vocabulary for love. Women
became masculine and could no longer give
birth to warmth or a simple caress with their
lips. Tongues were overweight from profanity
and the taste of nastiness. It settled over cities
like fog smothering everything in sight. My
ears begged for camouflage and the chance
to go to war. Everywhere was the decay of
how we sound. Someone said it reminded
them of the time Sonny Rollins disappeared.
People spread stories of how the air would
never be the same or forgive. It was the end
of civilization and nowhere could one hear
the first notes of *A Love Supreme.* It was as
if John Coltrane had never been born.

Love for a Song

J. Drew Lanham

Love is barter—bits of affection traded for pieces of adoration.

It is desire doled out on the whippoorwill's summer wanting. It is our craving for the meadowlark's ringing song—our longing for spring's greening from our sun-starved spirits down to our bare-toed roots. We seek the winding path and wander until we find the sweet spots— blackwater cypress swamp, tallgrass prairie sweep—the place where moonlight glancing off of tide-slicked stones makes us weep.

We want the wild soul and a shadow-dwelling wood thrush heaps it on us in self-harmonizing sonata—We revel in wildflower bloom—marvel in the migratory sojourns of birds dodging falling stars. Sink yourself deep in the dizzying dance of pollen-drunk bees. Find hope in the re-leaved canopies of the tallest trees. Wind and water—storm and surf—they can move us to other ends. Therein is the turn on. It's the honey sweet seduction. Nature asks only that we notice—a sunrise here—a sunset there. The surge, that overwhelming inexplicable thing in a swallow's joyous flight or the dawning of new light that melds heart and head into sensual soul in that moment of truly seeing—that is love.

Most Beautiful Accident: A Single Parent's Ode

Samantha Thornhill

I imagine the day you will ask me:
why is our life that Bill Withers song,
just the two of us?

You'll want to know why your father
isn't here disrupting our doorways,
off teaching you dangers I wouldn't dare.

How to tumble down hills with grace.
How to ride a bike with your hands
raised in prayer. Tossing you about

when I'm a stranger to fun, hoisting
you to ceilings with biceps twice as strong as mine
to make an airplane of you, superhero, rocket ship.

To my small hands, you're an astronaut.
Intrepid sojourner. You are universe
of brain with buckets of words.

So when you finally ask me
why is my daddy a faraway star? I'll say
beloved, you were his most beautiful accident.

Blinded him with your big bang,

divine astonishment. Demanding
little angel who arrived unannounced,

then remained. I know your father's love
doesn't feel like mine, but love
is like water, coming to us in multitudes.

It is rain beading across your hair,
snow melting on your lips. Avalanche.
Dew's slow delicacy. Hurts like hail.

I don't know if your father will ever come
around with his liquid eyes that I see in yours,
your exact dimples indenting his cheeks.

But should the day usher him here,
may the cup in your chest expand to accept
the potential oceans trickling from him.

His absence compels me to mother you
with the ardor of two — impossible joy!
When you fall asleep in the bassinet

you make of my arms, no room to lament:
I am your breath's one witness.
Your ear suctions to my chest.

Can you hear the hammers? My worker
heart's making a mansion of the world inside it —
your name kissed to its door.

How to Get Emotional Distance
When Voodoo Is Not an Option

Pamela L. Taylor

March in circles until his words
dizzy and fall out of your ears.
Heap those sighs and secrets
into a glass jar and leave
them out in the sun.
The bright light will purify
any microbes left behind.
Let your inner child gather your tears in buckets.
Wait three months for them to harden,
then sprinkle the salt rocks after the first snow.
If you live in a warm climate, move.
You have to retrain the amygdala
not to respond every time you pass by that place
where he first cupped your face
in his calloused hands. Try
counting backwards from one thousand,
but not in your mother tongue.
If none of this works, ask an Aquarian.
They'll tell you how to forget.

distant lover #1
[my michigan bed remix — for ellen g]

Brian Gilmore

dear lover. where you
once slept there are
books now. langston
hughes's *the weary blues*
& one about the kent
state shootings, 1970.
i don't read the books.
they are there to fill
the space. i hold hands
w/the books under the
covers, lover, think of them
as i doze off & dream of
you so far away. i imagine you
there beside me
reading in bed like
you did once; i
remember you saying
you would not be gone
long. it has been a while,
lover. there are a lot
of books there &
looks like many
more to come as the

space seems to get
larger & larger
the longer you are
gone though now
i have grown accustomed
for sleeping w/books.

last night, i began
to read the book
about how the
president once had
some students
murdered at kent
state university &
no one went to jail.
i met a woman once
who was a roommate
of one of the victims.
her room at kent
state suddenly
empty & quiet like
my room is each
night. she had nothing
to fill up the space. her
roommate dying every day
again, telling her she
would be back soon, she

was going to an anti-war
rally.

i have books &
your promise, lover, that
you will return, lay next
to me & read some-
thing or do nothing
at all but be here, alive
& in the big space you
created when you
departed. even
as i try to pretend
i can replace you
w/some books.

WHERE I'M FROM

Butter

Elizabeth Alexander

My mother loves butter more than I do,
more than anyone. She pulls chunks off
the stick and eats it plain, explaining
cream spun around into butter! Growing up
we ate turkey cutlets sauteed in lemon
and butter, butter and cheese on green noodles,
butter melting in small pools in the hearts
of Yorkshire puddings, butter better
than gravy staining white rice yellow,
butter glazing corn in slipping squares,
butter the lava in white volcanoes
of hominy grits, butter softening
in a white bowl to be creamed with white
sugar, butter disappearing into
whipped potatoes, with pineapple,
butter melted and curdy to pour
over pancakes, butter licked off the plate
with warm Alaga syrup. When I picture
the good old days I am grinning greasy
with my brother, having watched the tiger
chase his tail and turn to butter. We are
Mumbo and Jumbo's children despite
historical revision, despite
our parent's efforts, glowing from the inside
out, one hundred megawatts of butter.

Our People II

CM Burroughs

All cousins know the electric slide/how
to spell/despite the stink of it/chitterlings
or chitlins/the odor of pig feet or catfish
under a steam of vinegar/believe
blood is the most important thing/bring
family up for better or worse/better
the family or bemoan who just
won't do right/learn early the
power fist/dap/pound/and running
man/invent glorious ways to say
"brother" with intricacies of hands/we
cool/give elders their due/cull histories
in quilts/set records/set beats/set
rights/set Black Jesus/love our tannin
skin/drown yowls in jazz/watch blocks
bristle heat/in the hundreds/it's past
sundown/Mecca's everywhere now.

The Blue Dress

Her blue dress is a silk train is a river

is water seeps into the cobblestone streets of my sleep, is still raining

is monsoon brocade, is winter stars stitched into puddles

is good-bye in a flooded, antique room, is good-bye in a room of crystal
    bowls

and crystal cups, is the ring-ting-ring of water dripping from the mouths

of crystal bowls and crystal cups, is the Mississippi River is a hallway, is leaks

like tears from windowsills of a drowned house, is windows open to

waterfalls

is a bed is a small boat is a ship, is a current come to carry me in its arms

through the streets, is me floating in her dress through the streets

is only the moon sees me floating through the streets, is me in a blue dress

out to sea, is my mother is a moon out to sea.

127

Owed to the Plastic on Your Grandmother's Couch

Joshua Bennett

Which could almost be said
to *glisten,* or glow,
like the weaponry
in heaven.
Frictionless.
As if slickened
with some Pentecost
-al auntie's last bottle
of anointing oil, an ark
of no covenant
one might easily name,
apart from the promise
to preserve all small
& distinctly mortal forms
of loveliness
any elder
African American
woman makes
the day she sees sixty.
Consider the garden
of collards & heirloom
tomatoes only,
her long, single braid
streaked with gray

like a gathering
of weather,
the child popped
in church for not
sitting still, how even that,
they say, can become an omen
if you aren't careful,
if you don't act like you know

all Newton's laws
don't apply to us
the same. Ain't no equal
& opposite reaction
to the everyday brawl
blackness in America is,
no body so beloved
it cannot be destroyed.
So we hold on to what
we cannot hold.
Adorn it
in Vaseline, or gold,
or polyurethane wrapping.
Call it ours
& don't
mean owned.
Call it just
like new,
mean *alive.*

On Mother's Day

Frank X Walker

I'm going to pretend
that mine ain't dead,
that she's just quarantined.

Because she was a nurse
I know she'd be very serious
about social distancing,
hand washing, and the wearing
of masks.

So me and my siblings would
probably plant ourselves
six feet apart
in her backyard,
so that when she got up to
open her blinds and stepped out
onto her balcony
into the sunshine,
we'd all be sitting there
in our lawn chairs, smiling.

Somebody would lead us
in a song, which we'd sing
badly but with all our hearts.

She would blow us kisses
and rain down I love yous.

We'd linger until she made us go
or some other mother's day
pulled us away.

Folks are going to be salty
and complain all day about not
getting to hug their mamas.

Believe me when I tell you,
I really understand.

A Twice Named Family

Traci Dant

I come
from a family
that twice names

its own.
One name
for the world.

One name
for home.
Lydi, Joely, Door,

Bud, Bobby, Bea,
Puddin, Cluster, Lindy,
Money, Duddy, Vess.

Yes,
we are
a two-named family

cause somebody
way back knew
you needed a name

to cook chitlins in.
A name
to put your feet up in.

A name
that couldn't be
fired.

A name
that couldn't be
denied a loan.

A name
that couldn't be
asked

to go
through anyone's
back door.

Somebody way back
knew we needed names
to be loved in.

Another Homecoming

Jarita Davis

This picture was taken before the guests left
before my grandfather loosened his tie
buttoned his jacket back on the hanger
and smoothed the lapels flat with his thick hands.

In this moment, the house is filled with people
and neither the sofa nor the photo
can hold him, his smile, and the questions
from his daughters on either side.

Although she is still a girl
there is barely room for my mother
in this photo. There is her right knee,
her dark, bent braid, and bright eyes.

My aunt knows to fold her hands in her lap
and that the party is not for her.
She watches her father carefully,
guessing how long he'll stay.

Magnitude and Bond

Nicole Terez Dutton

More than anything, I need this boy
so close to my ears, his questions

electric as honeybees in an acreage
of goldenrod and aster. And time where

we are, slow sugar in the veins
of white pine, rubbery mushrooms

cloistered at their feet. His tawny
listening at the water's edge, shy

antlers in pooling green light, while
we consider fox prints etched in clay.

I need little black boys to be able to be
little black boys, whole salt water galaxies

in cotton and loudness — not fixed
in stunned suspension, episodes on hot

asphalt, waiting in the dazzling absence
of apology. I need this kid to stay mighty

and coltish, thundering alongside
other black kids, their wrestle and whoop,

the brightness of it—I need for the world
to bear it. And until it will, may the trees

kneel closer, while we sit in mineral hush,
together. May the boy whose dark eyes

are an echo of my father's dark eyes,
and his father's dark eyes, reach

with cupped hands into the braided
current. The boy, restless and lanky, the boy

for whom each moment endlessly opens,
for the attention he invests in the beetle's

lacquered armor, each furrowed seed
or heartbeat, the boy who once told me

the world gives you second chances, the boy
tugging my arm, saying *look,* saying *now.*

튀기 (Twigi)

Gary Jackson

Not every mulatto is created
equal. Some get heckled
on subway cars, lynched or celebrated
in tickertape parades. My mother can't speak

a lick of Korean and doesn't
give a damn, never says mulatto
but calls both of us mutts,
though I can't pass for shit but black:
ask the audience as I stroll in

late. We could use a Hines Ward
to show us the way — tell the boys
shouting *twigi* on the subway
all of us are animals, are hybrid

of body, of place. Mornings
I dream of kinked hair and cry.
My mother's mother forgets
who we are, speaks Korean over
our heads, lost in language.
My mother only nods,
exhausted. I know few words,
my tongue full of friction. *Say*

omma, I say, raise us
back into memory,
into word, into place. Once

a woman pressed into the pink
nailbeds of my fingers,
told me she could see
my blood. My mother
is mistaken for Hawaiian,
for Indian, for everything
but what she is. When I tell her
I'll have no children,
she says *then I guess we'll be
the only two left.* Somewhere
we are understood. My mother
opens her mouth.

For the Healing

Marlanda Dekine

Blessed loves, I offer future
children and their children who have your wild feet
running in lush palms without a reason or care. I believe
in the possibility of the blood-veined river emerging from your eyes
in this old photograph. I am not dead even though I have wished for it.
You show me that I am not dead.

I offer you everything that makes me smile
bright as the sun. I give you an old tire filled with collard greens
and the cackle of your great-great grand's laughter.

In this one-acre field where everything grows, I smell your quilts
and wonder about your secrets while I say all of your names.
I feel your hands trembling. The flesh of my flesh,
I offer you mine.

Inheritance

Tyree Daye

My mother will leave me her mother's deep-black
cast-iron skillet someday,
                                    I will fry okra in it,
weigh my whole life on its black handle,
lift it up to feel a people in my hand.
I will cook dinner
for my mother on her rusting, bleached stove
with this oiled star.
My mother made her body crooked
all her life to afford this little wooden blue house.
I want her green thumbs

wound around a squash's neck

to be wound around my wrist

telling me to stay longer. O what she grew with the dust

dancing in blue hours. What will happen to her body

left in the ground, to the bodies in the street,

the uncles turned to ash on the fireplace mantles

the cousins we've misplaced?

How many people make up this wound?

No one taught my mother how to bring us back to life,

so no one taught me.

O what we gather and O Lord

bless what we pass on.

Mule

Sharan Strange

I sat in the high back chair facing your bed,
silence and the long day between us. I listened
for a sound of need from you, grown smaller,
almost lost to the shadows enclosing the room.
I was nine and brave, they said, to do this.

The cancer had attacked your throat and stomach.
I didn't know the pain you felt,
just that you were weak, could eat only liquids
drawn through a tube. How it reduced you
from the tough, angry grandfather who frightened us,
who shouted and cursed his wife,
gold-grey eyes glinting like a blade.

Before illness whittled you all the way down
to pride, you worked full days with a mule
hard-driven through the boss's land. You warned us
never to stand behind it, so I took its twitching,
pointed ears, unblinking eyes, and rooted stance
for stubbornness, disregard, connected this to you.

Only the whistle and tick of your lungs
answered that you were still there, not yet
become spirit under my patient gaze.

You never betrayed what surely was brokenness,
the suffering that consumed you
even before it ruined your body. For months
you held on, until school ended my vigil
and I woke one morning to hear you'd gone.

Hanging Laundry

Maritza Rivera

Of all the chores
I did as a child

the one I hated most
was hanging laundry.

Clotheslines, clothespins
a basket of wet tee shirts
towels and bed linens:
my penance.
I saw nothing wrong
with just tossing them all
into the dryer and letting them
tumble into submission

but my insistent grandmother
would just not have it.
Why waste the warmth of the sun
she knowingly asked. Smell the tropical
breeze in the sheets she proclaimed.

I would say she had a point except
for the sudden downpour that always

followed once everything was
neatly hung and almost dry.

Running to rescue
hanging laundry
from the tears of angels
seemed so useless.

Now, here I am so many years later
seeing words hang like laundry

watching them bask in the warmth
of an unsuspecting page awaiting
a cloudburst of ink.

The Painter

Opal Palmer Adisa

(for lloyd walcott)

he came into
our home
with furrowed brows
      seeking in his sister
      the parent
      he never had
this man   my uncle
looking nothing
like my mother
      no ready smile
      no burnt cork skin
         just a tentative artist
who knew the smell
of the kitchen
the feel of a knife
that unfolds a cabbage
      as well as acrylic brushes
      on canvas
         it wasn't his desire
         to prepare food
         for the rich to savour
         or to take on a wife

149

                    or sire sons & a daughter

                    who might need his support

all he really wanted

was to paint the landscape

so others might notice it

sketch tubby women

languishing under domesticity

carve gods from wood

and be an artist

Beloved, Or If You Are Murdered Tomorrow

Elizabeth Acevedo

For Jordan Davis

it's easy to forget a pot of beans when you are numb.
the burning crinkled my nose but I didn't stir,
so when you came home

after work asking, *did you hear the verdict?*
i can only tell you i forgot to lower the heat,
that the stovetop stained where the beans split open

and pushed out from their skins; the boiling pot
sputtering blue-black water i can't bring myself
to clean.

cubans call this meal moros y cristianos,
the black beans and white rice cooked harmoniously.
today I'm convinced the cuban who named it was being overly
optimistic.

we say a silent grace over plain white rice.
and i wonder if you, like me, pray for an unborn child
we've already imagined shot in the chest.

tonight, no music plays and for the first time since i

learned to cook i understand
a meal can be a eulogy of mouthfuls.

neither one of us scrubs the stove. some things
deserve to be smudged. ungleaming. remembered.

"Harold's Chicken Shack #35"

Nate Marshall

fried gizzards w/ fries

your dad orders it for you
& you are too young
to know what you'll have
to swallow &
too old to refuse food.

good sauce is equality
for all fowl. you know
this crunch & thickness
around your tongue.

what changes is texture.
gizzard is stubborn,
muscular. you grind your
teeth like nervous sleep
to eat. you push all the hard
down your throat, away
from your taste buds.

gizzard is a bird's first
stomach to help

the avian break down
what it consumes.

you too swallow difficult shit
like gizzards & if
you're lucky sauce
might help. & if you're not
praise anyway. gravel
is necessary food.

On Rampart & Canal

Nadir Lasana Bomani

there is no service on Sundays
only shadows that lie
like deacons who testify

our faces bawled up
like children on pews
during pastor's anniversary

it's so hot out here
a Muslim is fanning himself
with The Final Call

the street preacher's bullhorn
said the devil went in Popeyes
cuz it has central air

an old woman shakes her head
like loose change
in a collection plate

someone starts moaning a hymn
while we wait on the bus
till Jesus comes

Where I'm From

Nikki Grimes

I'm from fried okra, catfish and knish,
black-eyed peas, and pickles from the barrel.
I'm from Harlem, the Heights, and Pulaski Street,
my roots intersecting Ossining, Red Hook,
Southeast Queens, South Bronx, and the South.

I'm from rent-party innovation,
hawking fried chicken, potato salad
and mustard greens, if you please—
whatever legally allowed hustle it took
to keep the lights on.

I'm from tar-beach picnics, subway rides,
and sweltering nights sprawled on firescapes
hearing snatches of broken Yiddish,
Chinese, Italian, Nuyorican, Greek,
and ten kinds of Black-speak.

I'm from lilacs and the miracle of daisies
interrupting sidewalk cracks, preening purple.
I'm from hat-and-glove Sundays
and parading past pews in syncopation
singing, "This Little Light of Mine."

I'm from math-mad Bernice, James on strings,
and Grandma Mac, who'd fling zingers like
"Use your head for more than a hat rack!"
I'm from no home, foster home, and home again.
But mostly, I'm from the crackle of Now,
learning to bloom in the place I'm planted.

Inundated

Hayes Davis

After Watching Hurricane Katrina Coverage on CNN

What tides move in him? At what watermark
did survival instinct kick in? How much water
is too high for wading? At what pitch
of a baby's cry does the father think diapers
or food instead of too deep, too much wind? On film

his trudge out of the French Quarter Walgreens
will be labeled "looting," his visage, gait
indistinguishable (to the casual viewer)
from people clutching stereos, sneakers, alcohol,
any item the newsroom seems to suggest
black people grab first. But look closely,

see Huggies under his right arm—who can
know his story? Who wouldn't grab a 12-pack,
if the bad day that sends us to Scotch on a Tuesday
were strung together for months, for lifetimes,
if what a teenager makes working a summer job
had to feed a family, if healthcare, a house
were fleeting dreams? So look

again—he carries milk with the Huggies and he's
black and he might not have made it home but you
wouldn't, probably, have heard if he didn't so call him
father, or husband, maybe Larry, or Junior, handsome,
thoughtful, drenched, scared, but not "looter."

The Black Girl Comes to Dinner

Taylor Byas

We drive into the belly of Alabama,
where God tweezed the highway's two lanes
down to one, where my stomach
bottoms out on each brakeless fall.

Where God tweezed the highway's two lanes
with heat, a mirage of water shimmers into view then
bottoms out. On each brakeless fall,
I almost tell you what I'm thinking, my mouth brimming

with heat. A mirage of water shimmers into view then
disappears beneath your tires.
I almost tell you what I'm thinking, my mouth brimming
with blues. Muddy Waters' croon

disappears beneath your tires.
I want to say I'm nervous beneath a sky brilliant
with blues. Muddy Waters' croon,
the only loving I'm willing to feel right now, the only loving

I want. To say I'm nervous beneath a sky brilliant
enough to keep me safe means to face what night brings.
The only loving I'm willing to feel right now, the only loving
that will calm me — I need you to tell me I am

enough. To keep me safe means to face what night brings
to the black girl in a sundown town—
that will calm me. I need you to tell me I am
safe. That they will love me, that the night will not gift fire

to the black girl in a sundown town.
Your grandmother folds me into her arms and I try to feel
safe. That they will love me, that the night will not gift fire
are mantras to repeat as

your grandmother folds me into her arms. And I try to feel
grateful. But *get home before it's too late* and *watch out for the flags*
are mantras to repeat as
we drive into the belly of Alabama.

oh didn't they tell us we would all have new names when we decided to convert?

Nikia Chaney

we don't offer to spirits
    just because the opposite of romance
        is violence
            we don't put the table against the door
                where the piano should sit
                    we say that there placed is a rug
                    because the playing is only
                    passion and life is still life
                    water and
                      bend downs fitting
                          snug into
                        prayer
                    positions
                  we don't need no honey
              or plate of silver
            beeswax gold
            we don't need no joint
          or wail in the song
        we think that singing words
      without knowing the meaning
    and pretending it signifies
  will cover up us up, still pimping our
hungriness by hand

we don't need ham

we don't need hung greasy faces

or tightened things getting lost

in the heaviness of the back door

we will recite in dark houses

the fluid in the words,

the color lines in the front

our memories of home

and when in our quiet,

our need to make

a part of the same

causes us to hide

our hers here,

give our hims the scrawl and whip

we'll just pretend we didn't know that

a slave

ruins even this, that the nigga

wrapped still has so many ways left

to finger-stroke all that old pain

Richard Pryor and me

Curtis L. Crisler

It's a feeling of holiday inside,
'cause every time I'm with you
you aren't funny, have less pressure
to be that rocket on stage, breaking us
into two with those cut-'em-up skills
God signed you on for. When we're
rappin' I only hear your hurt shatter
like Bird sellin' another sax for smack,
knowin' he gon' be back to get his
love-baby mellow soother — knowin'
he got bills, and women, and music
to support and spoon. When it's us,
Rich, rappin' and talkin' 'bout how Bad
got us in trouble growin' up — we'll both
tell each other we didn't have to follow
Bad but he had a way of gettin' into us
gut. He'd puff his cheeks on harmonica,
get dizzy with his looseness for trouble,
and we'd come runnin' — he didn't have
one smooth Coltrane note in him. Nawh,
he'd play a cutthroat-crossroad-sweetness
and we loved to chat and shoot our wads
with that fallin' angel, 'cause we knew
how if he had bones they'd rattle like ours

and he'd love the pain he'd feel for being
human, unlike us—scared to love big,
to follow our insanities. We try to hide
in our botched prayers, want only good
things, things appealing to the eyes
of others, stuff we hope to handle
on the run, and things big, red,
popped bright in glare.

In my extremity

Mary Moore Easter

*—addressing Eliza Winston, Mississippi slave escaped to freedom
in Minnesota, 1860*

There you were, Eliza,
       gold from God in plain sight

No one had picked you up
       wiped the muck from the landscape of your face.

Gold, I tell you, left for me to find,
       to polish. I won't say *to own*—

we've had enough of that.

I'm no colonizer of your shores,
       no conqueror to whom you must submit,

rather, a mirror that reflects what it sees—
       the you that was me, the background that was your time

the spaces surrounding you where I'd rummage
       and find my own things.

Only grace could have offered

        this circumstance to me:

the overlooked coin of the realm, a prize

        for the one who picks it up,

recognizes a value previously unimagined.

        I feel anointed by the discovery of you

a realm at the beck and call of all that is fertile in me,

        my feet untethered to walk your fields

climb the mountains

        embossed under the black of your golden face.

The old folks would shout: *Do! Jesus!*

Ode to Sudanese-Americans

Safia Elhillo

basma & rudy were first   each holding
     a mirror in her arms where i could see
my face as their faces   & we pierced

our noses & wore gamar boba
     in our ears & everyone at the party
thought them hoop earrings   & in the new york years

i crowd smoky bars alongside ladin
     & shadin & majid & linda & nedal
atheel & amir & elkhair   & mo & mohammed & mo

& we are forever removing our shoes in each other's
     apartments   ashing cigarettes
into the incense burner   making tea

with the good dried mint our mothers taught us
     to keep in the freezer   next to the chili
powder from home   making songs & dinner

& jokes in our parents' accents   & i am funniest
     when i have two languages to cocktail
when i can say *remember* & everyone was there

the rented room at the middle school on sundays

       where our parents volunteered to teach us arabic

to watch us bleat   alef baa taa thaa   & text

our american boyfriends that we were bored

      & at restaurants everyone asks if we are related

& we say yes   we do not date because we are probably

cousins   we throw rent parties & project the video

      where albabil sing gitar alshoug & i am not

the only one crying   not the only one made & remade

by longing   the mutation that arabic makes of my english

      metallic noises the english makes in my arabic

we ululate at each other's weddings   we ululate at the club

& sarah & hana make the mulah vegan   & in english safia

      spells her name like mine but pronounces it

like *purified*   sews a patch of garmasees

to the back of my denim jacket   we wash our underwear

      in the sink & make group texts on whatsapp

we go home & take pictures of the pyramids

we go home & take pictures of the nile   we move

      to other cities & feel doubly diasporic

& your cousin's coworker's little sister emails me

a list of bigalas in oakland   brings me crates

of canned fava beans from her own parents'

basement   & i say sudanese-american & mean also

british sudanese   & canadian & australian & raised

in the gulf   azza & yousra & amani & yassmin

& it's true that my people are everywhere

the uncles driving taxis at the end of our nights

the pharmacist who fills my prescription

who is named for the mole denoting beauty

adorning her left cheek   guardian spirits of my every

hookah bar   of my every untagged photograph

of crop tops & short shorts   & pierced cartilage & tattoos

of henna & headscarves & undercuts & shaved heads

my tapestries   embroidered with hundreds

of little mirrors   glinting like sequins in the changing light

Demonstration

Chanda Feldman

At the county extension service in the old downtown,
I spent after-school hours in my mother's office —
the green-glass building next to the city farmers' market

held in the parking lot each week — the entrance lined
with dark-stained oak cabinets, quarts
of tomatoes, the perfectly suspended fruit-flesh

in red liquid. Men holding Chinese food cartons
of soil, like purses, from their gardens and farms.
The soil needing to be fixed, the levels adjusted,

they'd puzzle over results laid out like blueprints.
My mother, a home economics agent, working
upstairs in the demonstration hall and kitchen,

the double-burner stove tops, the steaming silver pots.
In her hairnet, a lab coat over her blazer and
satin blouse. I sat in the chairs for the audience

with my homework until she called me up
to the platform to dip pH sticks to read the acid
contents. I'd slip the skin off peaches, level tablespoons

of salt for brines. My mother taught me
each step: the maceration, the strawberry-rhubarb
slurry heating to frothing, the sugar thermometer

rising to the gelling temperature of precisely 220
degrees. My mother pouring the fruit into scalded jars,
the room billowing with sweetness.

R&B Facts

Nicholas Goodly

All mermaids are black
and only hunt sailor men
who talk that fucknoise

Egypt is the proud grandmother
of Harlem and she sits back in her chair
with a switch in her hand

There is a brother
and a sister somewhere
just right for every child

If no black boys were murdered we
would have voices that speak in song
and the music we'd make would birth storms

We all can walk on water
as long as we never said
no anti-black shit

If we lit a candle for every pain
hurled towards the trans community
whole planets would be up in smoke

If we planted a tree for every word
against women the ground
would lose sight of the sun

A dead child's name at the top of your lungs
like an earth-splitting lightning rod
has the power to remember them back

One in three black girls learn
to swim by being chased away from
the shallow end of a brown community pool

Two out of five black families know
death as that play cousin who sleeps over
under comforters on the living room floor

There are black hills that only grow
in the heat of the sun
made of thick curling hair

The ghosts of black slaves are waiting
in one big front room with good music
til their whole families are free

Melanin, it's been proven, has endured
more than any beam of steel

The greek goddess of peaceful resistance
has died in a long-burning fire
and is buried in a fruitless urn

Nina Simone was born
in the 15th Century, her crib
was the bottom of a full boat

The bigger the hoops,
the braver the body

Armpit hair is permanently sexy,
acrylic nails start fires
in a heavy heart

Melanin bleeds a softness
wetter than silk

No one survives Etta James

The strongest homes are built
on onyx brick on muscle
covered in charcoal skin

Melanin is a blessing
that is ours like gold
melting in our hands

Melanin is light on every
surface of the day

There is no color on earth
that is not some child's favorite

If every human stood shoulder to shoulder
it would make an iron castle
with beating veins between the walls

All of us laid head to head
is a river feeding an ocean
too black to swim

Dear Future Ones

Jacqueline Woodson

Dear Future Ones who do not understand
an old woman puzzling over January crocuses
and the delicate shoots of tulips poking through winter leaves
Winter leaves us
questioning the absence of snow.

A headshake, a sigh, a mind turning inside the past:
Twenty years on this planet and my daughter can count
snowstorms lived through
on a single hand. Oh Dear

Future Ones, I apologize

for decades of Styrofoam lunches eaten happily because the world
would always be the way
I knew it as a child. I apologize

from tin cans thrown into trashcans. For the many years I loved
helium-filled mylar balloons. I apologize for the time I bought
an expensive deodorant, desired because I could spray it instead
of rolling it on. I apologize for the magical thinking
that led me to believe this world as I knew it
would always be here and bred you into with my mind on
other freedoms cuz

how many dreams of freedom can a single body hold
now old, you see me back bent and frowning
grateful for iceless sidewalks all winter long
and terrified. Oh Dear Future

Ones. You do not know a world

that isn't already burning, a time when flowers bloomed in seasons
we understood (Because once there were seasons here in New York). Once
snow barricaded me into my childhood home. Brooklyn. Blizzard of '78.
We waited, my siblings and I, gleefully imagining a June thaw
the four of us skeletons
heartbreakingly remembered.
We're history, we said. As though
we already knew what was coming.
As though, Future Ones, we already saw you out there
reading about us and remembering snow.

Back to the Past

Amanda Gorman

At times even blessings will bleed us.

There are some who lost their lives
& those who were lost from ours,

Who we might now reënter,
All our someones summoned softly.

The closest we get to time travel
Is our fears softening,

Our hurts unclenching,
As we become more akin

To kin, as we return
To who we were

Before we actually were
Anything or anyone—

That is, when we were born unhating
& unhindered, howling wetly

With everything we could yet become.

To travel back in time is to remember

When all we knew of ourselves was love.

Stand

Ruth Forman

why so afraid to stand up?
someone will tell you
sit down?

but here is the truth
someone will always tell you
sit down

the ones we remember
kept standing

Reunion

Reginald Harris

Basquiat's on the back steps with my niece
helping her to draw a picture of us all,
tossing back gray dreadlocks as they fall
into his eyes. My Sister argues politics
with Martin and Coretta in the back yard
over ribs — Romare Bearden's cooking —
Malcolm puts his two cents in between
bites of peas and rice. My grandfather
flirts with Billie as they remember the old
days on The Avenue in West Baltimore. Pres
brushes off his pork pie hat and stands, offers
to get my grandmother something from
the dessert table. She declines, full from her
second helping Duke Ellington's homemade
apple pie. Essex and Joe Beam line dance with
Audre and Pat Parker while Assotto Saint,
Melvin Dixon and my partner critique
from the picnic table off to one side.
Shamefaced, my father shows up late,
as always, with Charlie Parker and Bud Powell in tow.
Where've you-all been? my mother asks.
She gets a kiss and sheepish grin, but no reply.

Blue Magic

Niki Herd

As she parted my hair into four, I was a poem
in need of revision, too small for wigs like

she and the sweet-scented churchwomen wore,
so I sat on the vinyl kitchen floor, my arms holding

tight to knees as she yanked away
nappy coils and pressed them into ponytails

of dark ribbon. On Saturday afternoons, the kitchen
doubled as beauty shop, the gas stove an incense burner

smoking hot combs, curling rods and hair. Gladys sat
in a black lacquered chair, paid on lay-a-way from working

in the backs of restaurants and cleaning the insides
of toilets for white folks. It was honest work

for an honest person trying to make it in the world
and have a little left over. How happy she was

that one morning to place under the Christmas tree
my very own doll, one to sit with over the weekends

and do its hair. And I wonder how she felt when I
demanded she return the nylon haired plastic doll

for a white one. I didn't want something that needed
a grandmother, that needed hot combs and hair grease.

Sometimes you can watch a person age, the face
displays the cinematic reel of history, of white sheets,

burnt cross and blackface. She returned the doll
and I remember her more silent than usual. At that

moment in the car I could have been any girl, from
el barrio or the hood or the rez, any brownish girl riding

with her grandmother as the car inches away from the store lot,
families coated and gloved rushing with bags to and fro,

snow falling and eyes facing forward, while each
wiper on the windshield drags itself along—

Antebellum

Gregory Pardlo

Unfinished, the road turns off the fill
from the gulf coast, tracing the bay, to follow
the inland waterway. I lose it in the gritty
limbo of scrub pine, the once wealth
— infantile again, and lean — of lumber barons,
now vested in the state, now sanctuary for renegades
and shamans, for pot growers and moonshiners,
the upriver and clandestine industries that keep
mostly to themselves.

Misting over a lake-front terraced lawn, evening's pink
tablet, japanning lawn and lake, magnolia leaf,
ember easing, dips and gives gilt to the veiled
nocturne vanishing in the view: the hint of maison
through the woods faint as features pressed on
an ancient coin. Swart arms of live oaks that hag
their bad backs surreptitiously, drip Spanish moss
like swamp things out of where a pelican taxis limp-
legged across the lake, pratfalls awkward as a drunk
on a bike. The bat above me, like a flung wristwatch.

Pastoral

Natasha Trethewey

In the dream, I am with the Fugitive
Poets. We're gathered for a photograph.
Behind us, the skyline of Atlanta
hidden by the photographer's backdrop—
a lush pasture, green, full of soft-eyed cows
lowing, a chant that sounds like *no, no. Yes,*
I say to the glass of bourbon I'm offered.
We're lining up now—Robert Penn Warren,
his voice just audible above the drone
of bulldozers, telling us where to stand.
Say "race," the photographer croons. I'm in
blackface again when the flash freezes us.
My father's white, I tell them, *and rural.*
You don't hate the South? they ask. *You don't hate it?*

Southern History

Natasha Trethewey

Before the war, they were happy, he said,
quoting our textbook. (This was senior-year

history class.) *The slaves were clothed, fed,*
and better off under a master's care.

I watched the words blur on the page. No one
raised a hand, disagreed. Not even me.

It was late; we still had Reconstruction
to cover before the test, and—luckily—

three hours of watching *Gone with the Wind.*
History, the teacher said, *of the old South*—

a true account of how things were back then.
On screen a slave stood big as life: big mouth,

bucked eyes, our textbook's grinning proof—a lie
my teacher guarded. Silent, so did I.

Nelsons
(On the Road 1957)

Marilyn Nelson

Daddy's handsome: uniform, new haircut.
But the travel baby bed in our seat
crowds me and Jennifer. We kept asking,
"Are we there yet?" every few endless miles,
until Daddy shouted, "HEY!" and braked. We braced
ourselves. We skidded, turned, and spit gravel
up a long driveway ending at a barn.
Barking dogs. Mama whispered Daddy's name.
A light-haired man came out. He calmed the dogs,
and looked at Daddy with inquiring eyes.
Daddy called, "Hello! We saw your mailbox!
We're Nelsons, too! I fly B-52s!
Would you mind letting my girls see your farm?"
That's why I'm here petting this stupid cow.

Accents (After Denice Frohman)

Yvette R. Murray

Sistah, my Mama has the sky in her mouth too

She carries beautiful Hausa, rhythmic Igbo and exquisite Yoruba

All smashed into one gumbo called Gullah.

Gullah: The language of survival.

In muck of rice fields

and muck of this republic

It flows with a rhythm so deep, deep, deep

It has to be eaten,

like all good gumbo should,

with cornbread.

We know that the beauty of this creole

is living on nothing

Thriving in mist

Governed by the moon itself,

Gullah

pounds the shore

like the tide

dragging grains of sand

to build islands elsewhere.

Hidden deep within our throats,

language of rebellion,

seen in the eyes,

heard in the tilt of a chin,

My Mama brought it to me

with the pride of bare feet.

We are yet

being used

bought, sold, traded

packed, shipped, and pilfered

for

now, poachers take Gullah like ivory

and put her on their trinkets to sell.

The Mystery Man in the Black Hat Speaks

Quincy Troupe

I am the spirit of the dead African man lost in the Atlantic during storms and murders crossing those terrible waters during the Middle Passage. My spirit though mixed in a mélange with blood of Cherokees and the spirits of Tom Ridge Tom Ross the Apache warrior Geronimo the Sioux Chief Sitting Bull and the Shawnee Chief Tecumseh and his younger brother Tenskwatawa the one-eyed prophet and a whole lot of others. I rise up out of the ground out of the rivers walk and cut through mist fog tornado clouds hurricane winds come out of the ground from cracks of earthquakes the flaming lava of volcanoes and come here to this Mississippi River not far from Cahokia where the ancestors came upriver from the gulf and built those pyramids there to spite the white man. So I double/cross through the upside-down question mark of this here shining steel arch down here on the levy of Sad Louis and emerge from behind the polished steel and come out to greet you here to bring you a message but I can see you ain't ready yet so eye done changed my mind and I'm gon' walk back through the roiling rolling fog and mist until you ready to talk to me righteously because I am the voodoo spirit of African Indian double-take of cross-fertilization here in this cruel conflicted place called America. I am the double-back winding swamp snake who can cure these tortured spirits living here in this hellfire & brimstone place if only they will listen to me tell them the righteous truth. But until then I will come and go as I please as I want to sliding through the night with my mojo bone and juba shaking feather and appear whenever and wherever it suits me in

199

my black hat and black cape sometimes riding a black horse and carrying a black whip that is my tongue that cracks and slips through the language we speak like a black mamba snake I move fast as an out-of-control brushfire strike deadly quick as a drone's exploding missile and then I'm gone just like that in the blinking flash of an eye.

The I Be Tree

truth thomas

I be

pirate prints

on African fingers.

I be slave and Cherokee.

I be Ben Hur Ave and

Strawberry Plains, a colored

only survivor. I be Avon Nyanza,

Carrie Bell Cole, I be Five Points,

clothespins and Knoxville. I be

Mamaw and Papaw, Grandfather

Erskin, shoeshines on Central and Vine.

I be son of Carridella—who shouldn't have

made it past 3—pneumonia, paralysis, fever

and tears. I be prayers hanging over a crib.

I be Seven Day Episcopal Baptist Holiness

AME. I be segregated popcorn dropped in

Gay Street movie seats. I be picture frames for

fathers. I be women raising men. I be Mother

Macklin's crackling bread, her bat catchin rats in

the pantry. I be uncles fightin Klansmen, giving as

good as they got. I be package stores and cigarettes,

holy birds and hymnals. I be hound dogs yawning

porches. I be lightning bugs in jars. I be trailers tied

to bumpers. I be U Hauled to DC. I be battling out on

Eastern Ave. I be afro picks with fists. I be rent strikes,

roaches, PF Flyers, James Brown on "the one." I be tank

treads rolling, U Street smoking, Coretta's assassinated smile.

I be bruises like plums on my mother's arms—a gift from my

second non-father. I be nails in his cheeks, teeth in his back,

as she gave as good as she got. I be the panther

in her eyes that stopped the attacks.

Yes

I be

all that.

We not crazy, we feeling irie

Arisa White

She rolls my locks like a spliff. Her dreadlocks thick
as cattails weep to her shoulders.

It's the 80s. When my mother and I walk the streets,
strangers avoid us as if we carry a shitting stench.

Leaning into her chest, the scent of her skin
sweetens my air like a frankincense burn.

She tells me to say my ABCs, massages my head
until my scalp absorbs lavender oil.

Our hair's mat and nap is treason against granny's
straightened bob and auntie's permed curls.

They say, *No little girl should have her hair like that;
what would people think?*

My mother sings as if her tongue were raised
alongside the sea's echo.

Her Jamaican accent acquired from Rasta associations
brings tide to steel of city living.

With the complaint that vegetarianism is starvation,
my aunt threatens to call child welfare.

What social worker would mistake grating coconuts for *ital*,
squatting on the kitchen floor, as an act of neglect?

The record player wakes Beres Hammond's vinyl silence;
his voice a warm rain when the skin asks for cooling.

She has played the same song all week. She lifts me from her lap
and gestures to dance. I spin my skirt into a parasol.

She stands, moves with waves beneath her,
an island body lit by uncovered bulbs.

I join her muted march, our locks in pendulum sway.
We two trees in the coming of winter, putting up resistance.

DEVOTIONS

His Presence

The presence of God is like a flame
  melting the wax beneath it,

like the feet of the wind
  pounding the mountains to rubble,

like floodwater
  flowing down the slopes,

like the white devouring of glaciers
  through the green of river valleys,

like the precise incisions
  of hill rice growers

shaping generations of steps
  on the mountainsides.

This is the presence of the Lord;
  thanks be to God.

You Are Not Christ

Rickey Laurentiis

New Orleans, Louisiana

For the drowning, yes, there is always panic.
Or peace. Your body behaving finally by instinct
alone. Crossing out wonder. Crossing out
a need to know. You only feel you need to live.
That you deserve it. Even here. Even as your chest
fills with a strange new air, you will not ask
what this means. Like prey caught in the wolf's teeth,
but you are not the lamb. You are what's in the lamb
that keeps it kicking. Let it.

Conjecture on the Stained-Glass Image of White Christ at Ebenezer Baptist Church

Marcus Wicker

For in the one Spirit we were all baptized into one body—Jews or
Greeks, slaves or free—and all were made to drink of one Spirit.
—1 Corinthians 12:13

If in his image made am I, then make me a miracle.

Make my shrine a copper faucet leaking everlasting Evian to the masses.

Make this empty water glass a goblet of long-legged French wine.

Make mine a Prince-purple body bag designed by Crown Royal

for tax collectors to spill over & tithe into just before I rise.

If in his image made am I, then make my vessel a pearl Coupe de Ville.

Make mine the body of a 28-year-old black woman

in a blue patterned maxi dress cruising through Hell on Earth, TX

again alive. If in his image made are we, then why

the endless string of effigies?

Why so many mortal blasphemes?

Why crucify me in HD across a scrolling news ticker, tied

to a clothesline of broken necks long as Time?

Is this thing on? Jesus on the ground. Jesus in the margins.

Of hurricane & sea. Jesus of busted levees in chocolate cities.

Jesus of the Middle East (Africa) & crows flying backwards.

Of blood, on the leaves, inside diamond mines, in under-

developed mineral-rich countries. If in your image made are we,

the proliferation of your tie-dyed hippie doppelgänger

makes you easier to daily see. & in this image didn't we make
the godhead, slightly stony, high enough to surf a cloud?
& didn't we leave you there, where, surely, paradise or
justice must be meted out? Couldn't we see where water takes
the form of whatever most holds it upright? If then this
is what it's come down to. My faith, in rifle shells.
In Glock 22 magazine sleeves. Isn't it also then how, why,
in a bucket shot full of holes, I've been made to believe?

Condition: If the Garden of Eden Was in Africa

DéLana R. A. Dameron

Having learned
they had been lied to;
having tasted bitter knowledge
and flirted with forked-tongue
soothsayer who sought to make a deal
from their flesh — after it was too late
to renege, who walked first
through that gate no longer blind —
having seen what they were leaving,
what would still be theirs,
and not dust and desert
if they could have stayed?

Offertory

Chris Abani

You can smell a humid rain miles before the water

envelopes you, a hot smell, ripe as a swamp.

This is the day, you say, the cusp of return, restitution for sin.

The animal is calm under your hand, but still a throb of life.

To measure the distance a knife travels

in wonder toward the neck,

or something like fear, or regret, or even, say, delight.

In the shade of your shrine, your lineage

ghosts between light and shade.

Though we know grief cannot raise the dead,

we speak the spells nonetheless.

Nothing outlasts the arc of the heart.

No intelligence can reason away sorrow.

Still, gin cupped in prayer is a fragile gift.

We speak in libation to remember.

grief

toni blackman

make your grief earn its place
don't allow it to take up space without
gifting you something
your existence, your presence a present
be present
make sure your grief is worth the pain

tell your tears what to do
cry on purpose, with deliberate intention
have your tears water your dreams
so that something beautiful blooms in their absence

allow them to flow, never imprison them
too many are drowning from the inside
suffocating from emotional suppression
internalizing oppression

free your/self imposed limitations
set your higher heights for your vibration

let those tears moisten your vocal chords
then moan
all ancestral-like, moan

like black grandmothers in the church pew
moan, make noise
loud enough for the heavens to hear you above
this is not the time for silence

sallie ledbetter: a mother's hymn

Tyehimba Jess

when the black boy climbs out of my womb:

how to peel dynamite from his bones?

how to strip tornado's hum from his ears?

how to weed graveyard from his garden of tongue?

what rainbow of prayer to pull between teeth?

how to blind him from liquor's sun of stupor?

how to sow whisper into his hurricane of hips?

what blizzard of plea to freeze his tremor of feet?

how to lift him from streetlight blaze?

which revengeful breast fed him this poison?

which breast gilded his mouth with song?

My Father's Geography

Afaa Michael Weaver

I was parading the Côte d'Azur,
hopping the short trains from Nice to Cannes,
following the maze of streets in Monte Carlo
to the hill that overlooks the ville.
A woman fed me pâté in the afternoon,
calling from her stall to offer me more.
At breakfast I talked in French with an old man
about what he loved about America—the Kennedys.

On the beaches I walked and watched
topless women sunbathe and swim,
loving both home and being so far from it.

At a phone looking to Africa over the Mediterranean,
I called my father, and, missing me, he said,
"You almost home boy. Go on cross that sea!"

Sunday Poem

Joel Dias-Porter

for Ernesto, Brandon, Gary, and Renée

Lilley and I discuss a famous poem
which claims "Death is the mother of beauty,"
walking up First St. NW, just before
the last streaks of sun leak from the sky
above Renée's crib where we hold
our Black Rooster workshop.
I recall holding Ronald
early one church morning after
he got shot on his Mama's front steps —
how his eyes rolled like white marbles —
and begin wondering if the same logic
which produced that poem,
also perhaps implied the mushrooms
that clouded Hiroshima or Nagasaki?
Someone yells from an idling green van,
we look over and it's Melvin who used
to have dreads and clown about "The Killer"
when he was in my WritersCorp workshop
at Lorton Prison. Only now he's free
and has shaved his head. The light changes
and Melvin pulls off, so I tell Gary
"The Killer" joke and we laugh so hard

I almost miss the carnations placed
by the stop sign, or the wine bottles
arranged around them like decorations
in a nigga cemetery. Gary
says "Damn" just as I peep the blown-up
photograph held to the fire-box
by maybe half a roll of Scotch tape.
And what does it mean that the name
"Pooh" is printed in blue ball-point above
a brother crouching as I once crouched
in nightclubs posing for five dollar pictures?
Perhaps I recognize this kid flossing
Nikes that match his Nautica jacket,
because I passed him or someone
similar to him coming out
of the liquor store on the corner
of Florida Ave last Friday, when I stopped
to cop a bottle of Evian and
some Juicy Fruit. Their hair was cornrowed
and they cradled a beer in one hand,
while holding the door with the other.
And I pray *i* mumbled "Thanks," before the door
swung shut. There are two dates, neither
of which are dried fruit, scrawled under
the feet in the photo and I lean in to nose
one of the carnations. Now my eyelashes
clump as I recall stringing Ronald's
Nikes from the power lines above

his mother's crib. I pull my lucky geode
from a front pocket and set it down
near the bottles, then step back
under a sky that's gone all black
to ponder what Stevens might've written,
if the Beauty he so believed in
only sometimes believed in him.

I Could Eat Collard Greens Indefinitely

Alice Walker

I could eat collard greens
Indefinitely.
Every morning
I think this
As I place a few
Flat, home grown
Leaves
In my pan.
Pan, not pot.
For we have graduated
To speed, to rapt
Anticipation;
To a stirring
Sensuousness
That satisfies
My sense of passion;
& I want them
Inside me
Like the lover
Of my body
That
They are.
Their green goodness
Beckoning me
To rise.

The Gray Mare

Afaa Michael Weaver

With my left hand on her shoulder, my right hand
sliding across her back, I take in the smell of horse,
pushing my nose into her hair, rubbing against her
until she leans into me as if she wants to fall asleep
inside the love, stroking and stroking until her coat
has the brightness of new starlight, the morning
sounds the brood of beagle puppies in the barn,
the calves out in the back pasture trying to nurse.
Up and down the length of her side, one hand
to steady myself, one hand to measure the distance
inside a wish to be one with horse and landscape,
the way the sky feels when I lift my hands, stretch
my arms apart to split the clouds and know a horse
is the fragile piece of God, the one divine bit of flesh
that fell to earth with us, took on the definite bones
of being mortal to be what we cannot be, strong
where we are weak, weak where we are strong so
we become the one thing when I stretch my hands
over the back of this gray mare and we are saved.

Easter Prayer, 2020 A.C.

Frank X Walker

All powerful Black Jesus,
please protect my brothers and sisters
and their families and friends
when they gather together, illegally,
to enjoy Easter Dinner and the Sabbath.

May they pass around the sanitizer
after holding hands in prayer.

May whoever is lifting up your name
be wearing a mask correctly, oh Lord.

May any pork that touches their lips
not mess with their blood pressure.

Hide the salt, sweet Jesus, and please grant
them the vision to bring at least one sugar-free
dessert, some diet sodas, and unsweetened tea.

Strengthen them for their fight against
that devil diabetes and all cancers, Lord.

Thank you for their on-time unemployment
checks, Medicaid, and Obama Care.

Help them choose wisely if the choice is between
the cable and the light bill, and their life insurance.

And if it is your will to take all they asses
because they refuse to believe COVID-19 is real,
let this be the best meal they ever ate, Lord.

And take them all on the same day, so that they
may offer comfort to each other in the hospital

and allow the rest of us to endure only one
drive-through service.

Amen.

Tell Them What You Want

Jabari Asim

I want Gods with groins.

I want my Gods sticky and wet. I want Gods with bedroom eyes.

I want my Gods quick and dirty and wholly unashamed.

I want Gods who grunt and touch themselves.

I want Gods who won't double-cross me.

I want Gods who say to me, did you really think you could get over
without us?

I want Gods who want me back, who say hey, son, *we were just
thinking about you.*

I want Gods who anoint their elbows with moisturizer.

I want Gods with alabaster dust under their heels, floating up
between their black toes like powdered sugar.

I want Gods with stars in their crotches.

I want Gods who chant and wiggle, gods with breasts and big backsides.

I want Gods who hum and snap their long dark fingers. I want Gods
who wink at me when
I look in the mirror.

I want Gods who say holy water is wherever I wash.

I want Gods doing the Watusi on the banks of the river, at the edge of
the city, at the foot of the hill, in the middle of the mall.

I want Gods whose lips glisten with pot liquor.

I want Gods who cook cornbread in a cast-iron skillet.

I want Gods whose kisses taste like yams.

I want Gods who talk back at the movie screen.

I want Gods who speak in drum.

I want Gods who will wake. me. up.

I want Gods who say your mind is your church.

I want Gods who say you won't find us in a book.

I want Gods who say your own stories are enough.

I want Gods who say don't look up, look around.

I want Gods who insist that here is hereafter, hereafter is here.

I want Gods who whisper in my ear the very thing I need to remember:

Resist.

Devotions

All night you pace between our bed and another
room in the house, fetching glasses of water
when you mean shots of gin. The candle
doesn't catch your naked body—a leg, the cut
of stubble—only the shadow of its leaving,
the whole of you uncontainable like the moon,
its kissable face and its darker chambers.

Mary offers her mangled son, a matchmaker,
from the dollar-store votive by the bed.
(Other nights John the Baptist rolls his eyes at me.)
You're the one who stayed, or
at least never left. You stay because of hard rain,
or dead magnolia on the drive; or is it custom
for the wounded to care for the wounded?

Where are you? I need a solitary room
with you in it. Wall me in. Lie down on me.

Wanderlust

Remica Bingham-Risher

Where you headed?

> *Maybe North*

Where you been?

> *Yonder, hard times, a street none name*

Where you sleep?

> *In the woods, with others*

Where's your kin?

> *Daddy left with the union, most of us scattered: everywhere*

Where this road lead?

> *A free town*

Who all over there?

> *Right many*

Will you walk til night?

Long as I can

What you trying to find?

A mountain like a bridge

Who told you of it?

My love, in the dark

Does the road whisper now?

Whispers and sings

Are many children on it?

Some so small, they might not remember

Can we pray on that?

That and a safe journey

God come by here?

Could be a stranger, could be you Him

RACE RAISE RAGE: THE BLACKENED ALPHABET

To Racism

In recognition of the looming extinction
as prison-for-profit marched
our next millionth man to jail,
we took matters into our own hands,

propelled you to the nearest
dumpster and threw you in.
We were sick to death of you
peeking out from under white, connotative

sheets, trying to play the invisible man.
We would have rid ourselves of you for good
if it hadn't been for all that whimpering.
A good Samaritan (a lawyer, I think)

reached in, sewed you up as tight as pigskin,
and siphoned you back out onto the streets.
When I saw you again in the furtive
shadows you were cradling a black doll

like the one Daddy bought for me.
I swear I thought you'd had a come-to-Jesus
moment—til I looked harder and saw
your Mickey-Mouse minstrel-gloves,

blackface slathered on thick as Hershey's....
And then the crow cawed and I
heard twin sockets shrieking
where the doll's eyes should have been.

And this poem is familiar to people who don't read
poetry, who don't know it's not supposed to work
like this.... which is why I wrote it,
which is why it will be read.

242

The Blackened Alphabet

Nikky Finney

While others sleep
My black skillet sizzles
Alphabets dance and I hit the return key
On my tired But ever jumping eyes
I want more I hold out for some more
While others just now turn over
shut down alarms
I am on I am on
I am pencilfrying
sweet Black alphabets
In an allnight oil

"I'm Rooting for Everybody Black"

—Issa Rae

Cortney Lamar Charleston

Everybody Black is my hometown team. Everybody Black
dropped the hottest album of the year, easy. Everybody Black
is in this show, so I'm watching. Everybody Black is in this movie,
so I'm watching. Everybody Black wore it better, tell the truth.
Everybody Black's new book was beautiful. How you don't
know about Everybody Black?! Everybody Black mad
underrated. Everybody Black remind me of someone I know.
I love seeing Everybody Black succeed. I hope Everybody Black
get elected. Everybody Black deserves the promotion more than
anybody. I want Everybody Black to find somebody special.
Everybody Black is good peoples. Everybody Black been through
some things. Everybody Black don't get the credit they're due. I met
Everybody Black once and they were super chill and down-to-earth.
I believe in Everybody Black. There's *something* about Everybody Black.

The Blue Seuss

Terrance Hayes

Blacks in one box

Blacks in two box

Blacks on

Blacks stacked in boxes stacked on boxes

Blacks in boxes stacked on shores

Blacks in boxes stacked on boats in darkness

Blacks in boxes do not float

Blacks in boxes count their losses

Blacks on boat docks

Blacks on auction

Blacks on wagons

Blacks with masters in the houses

Blacks with bosses in the fields

Blacks in helmets toting rifles

Blacks in Harlem toting banjoes boots and quilts

Blacks on foot

Blacks on buses

Blacks on backwood hardwood stages singing blues

Blacks on Broadway singing too

Blacks can Charleston

Blacks can foxtrot

Blacks can bebop

Blacks can moonwalk

Blacks can beatbox

Blacks can run fast too

Blacks on

Blacks and

Blacks on knees and

Blacks on couches

Blacks on Good Times

Blacks on Roots

Blacks on Cosby

Blacks in voting booths are

Blacks in boxes

Blacks beside

Blacks in rows of houses are

Blacks in boxes too

Dear Barbershop,

Chris Slaughter

> *Is this a barbershop? If we can't talk straight*
> *in the barbershop, then where can we talk straight?*
> —*Eddie Cedric*

I come from you: every argument, debate and dare—
every hand-me-down bet that taught me to run

from nothing while fading the world down small enough
to doubt. No one else understands the gravity

in the way a chair turns after a fight, and blood stains
hair and hardwood floors. Music somehow tells the story

better than us, mirrors turn away, but I saved
the dirt from my nails. I'm not hard currency

to you—anymore. I'm no longer steady handed and perfect for slang.
You say, with every chair in the shop full, "What happened to you man?

You even look at customers like they're not good enough anymore"
—but I'm made from discussion, contradiction, and cheap cognac. Cussing

in every sentence just to get points across the room. I'm a glass bottle on the ledge of some mantle that built a ship inside of itself (and the ghosts

    it holds).

I'm against the same grain as I've always been, believe in
the same sharp line and burn. I'm the same crazy bastard

that called the pizza man a racist, with mute Omar by my side
waving his arms—don't forget what hurts,

what makes our blood agree, how women come in alone
with their boys and listen to us go on about presidents, one-night-stand
sex,

and Kobe's fade-away; they listen to us throw *nigga* and *bitch* around
like natural terms of endearment— I just want my name back.

Before I Fire Her, The Therapist Asks *What IS It Like to Be a Black Woman HERE*

Aricka Foreman

I love your hair You always wear such *interesting* things What did you do before this Wow are you from Detroit What was that like Tell me what your thesis is about That sounds really powerful Your poem tonight was really intense You'll appreciate this, you know, since you're kind of ghetto You worked so hard you made it So what did you think about that Junot essay I'm suspicious of poems with an agenda, that have a certain aboutness Explain what you mean when you say risk I'm really uncomfortable I went to Detroit, well Dearborn, and it's amazing how cheap the houses are No, it's a really cool town Are you a Tigers fan That city is having a hard time, for sure I lived there once when I worked for Teach for America How do you feel about people who claim Detroit but aren't really from there I really love your hair Is your work always so intense That line is a little melodramatic I'm not as smart as you but I thought rape was about sex What do you mean it's hard to date I mean you're *here* Rap is about music let's not make it about race Oh come on, I only call people I love my nigga I don't mean this to sound racist but You don't seem like you date white guys but I love how our skin looks when I hold your hand and I like women who live a natural lifestyle and You're so well spoken Wow you've really read a lot Ithaca must be way different than what you're used to You can breathe now, you made it

A Piece of Tail

Teri Ellen Cross Davis

from their apartment's balcony
my girlfriends and I could see their pale skins
hear the clipped accents the soldiers were British
and drunk with money flowing the Kenyan women became

willing every stare every intoxicating
their tore shirts, teased skirts revealed panties
gyrated and taunted those English boys who'd never
seen chocolate breasts nipples tipped almost ebony

hips that rounded to such a swelling
you needed two hands to grab it all
but they'd heard how wild black cats can be
scratching backs lusty animals in a vaguely human skin

it brought me back to Ohio University's frat row
drunk white faces leering and eager to believe
emboldened voices calling out and I became afraid
I was that exotic again kin to these Kenyan women

and we were all dancing on bar table tops
for dollars or pounds whatever brown bodies go for these days

Why I Can Dance Down a Soul-Train Line in Public and Still Be Muslim

Aisha Sharif

My Islam be black.
Not that Nation of Islam
"Don't-like-white-folks"
kind of black. I mean my Islam be
who I am—black, born and raised
Muslim in Memphis, Tennessee,
by parents who converted
black. It be my 2 brothers
and 2 sisters Muslim too
black, praying at Masjid Al-Muminun,
formally Temple #55,
located at 4412 South Third Street
in between the Strip Club
and the Save-A-Lot black.
My Islam be bean pie black,
sisters cooking fish dinners
after Friday prayer black,
brothers selling them newspapers
on the front steps black, everybody
struggling to pay the mortgage back
Black.

My Islam be Sister Clara Muhammad School
black, starting each day
with the pledge of allegiance
then prayer & black history
black. It be blue jumpers
over blue pants, girls pulling bangs out
of their hijabs to look cute
black. My Islam be black & Somali
boys and girls, grades 2 through 8,
learning Arabic in the same classroom
cuz we only had one classroom
black. It be everybody wearing a coat inside
cuz the building ain't got no heat
Black.

My Islam be the only Muslim girl
at a public high school
where everybody COGIC asking sidewise,
What church you go to?
black. It be me trying to explain hijab
black, *No, I don't have cancer. No,*
I'm not a nun. No, I don't take showers
with my scarf on. No, I'm not
going to hell cuz I haven't accepted
Jesus Christ as my Lord and Savior
black. My Islam be riding on the city bus
next to crackheads and dope boys
black, be them whispering black,

be me praying they don't follow me home
Black.

My Islam don't hate Christians
cuz all my aunts, cousins,
and grandparents be Christian
black. It be joining them for Easter
brunch cuz family still family
black. My Islam be Mus-Diva
black, head wrapped up,
feathered and jeweled black. It be me
two-stepping in hijab and four-inch heels
cuz dancing be in my bones
Black.

My Islam be just as good as any Arab's.
It be me saying, *No, I ain't gonna pray
in a separate room cuz I'm a woman*
black. And, *Don't think I can't recite Quran too.*
Now pray on that black!

My Islam be universal
cuz black be universal.
It be Morocco and Senegal,
India and Egypt. My Islam
don't need to be *Salafi*
or *Sufi*. It don't have to be
blacker than yours black.
My Islam just has to be.

Fuck / Time

Inua Ellams

Once upon a time / Yo-Yo Ma / traveling through Botswana searching for music / crosses a local shaman singing / into the savannah / He rushes to notate the melody / Please Sing Again he requests / to which the shaman sings something else and explains / to the baffled Yo-Yo Ma that earlier / clouds had covered the sun and wild antelope grazed in the distance / But the dial of the world had twirled since / The antelopes had cantered into some other future / The clouds had gone / so the song had to change / had to slough off the chains us mortals clasp everything with / even our fluid wrists / The universe in fact is monstrously indifferent to the presence of man / We are small as moth wing fall / in an orchestra broad as galaxies / playing a symphony Time isn't bothered to fathom / It respects no constant and is always moving on

Beyoncé on the Line for Gaga

Morgan Parker

Girl you know you ain't that busy.
Without me   you're just two ears
stuffed with glitter.
      Spoken gun   your name
baby's first words when she enters
      swag up   covered in
gunmetal spandex, cigarettes for eyes.
Say my name, louder
      come into   these hips
and live. Let
platform heels tightrope curves,
      make Jiggaman jealous.
He runs the streets
I pour into them, weave first
fierce nymph of Texas
      holy in black.
You feel me? This booty
is smooth running water.
I shake   too thick for love,
push records like dimes,
rep the hustle   slick as legs.
I know you like that.
      I carry the hood up in this bling.
Soft brown fingers

got rocks for days. Lips glossed opening

      for a special purpose.

You say *Tell 'em B*

I open my legs, throw my shades on like,

Divas gettin' money.   Hard as the boys.

Give me all

your little monsters and I will burn them up.

Give me your hand

and I will let you back this up.

Tonight   I make a name for you.

Contemplating "Mistress," Sally in 2017

Chet'la Sebree

I was so much more because I was so much less —
list of lewd comments and epithets.

I was currency, chattel, animal
when he came to me mammal —

craving *the odor* I secreted,
biting my flesh with his teeth.

He would have had to put me first
to have named me in earnest —

scared of how someone with my skin
would have been seen by his kin.

Others took the liberty — made me
the *Dusky Sally* of drawings and songs.

None of them to ever know me:
girl, child, woman, mother;

confused, scared, alone
bone to bone

with the only man
I'd ever know —

in a teen dream fantasy
where I chose

to return to land I called home.
Not imagining daughter turned stranger,

dust of children abandoned on a mountain
to which I cannot return,

that I would become
reconstructed

versions of someone I don't know
in converted closets, movies, these poems,

because a sliver of pigment
kindled his ardent,

because I let a child make a decision
for this *extraordinary privilege.*

Mussels

Lucinda Roy

Having been mistaken once again for the other black couple in town,
we take our seats at the table. Name tags corrected, we order with the rest.
When the subject of race comes up during appetizers (for me
steamed mussels in white wine with tarragon; for you nothing—
as usual, you're saving yourself for dessert) I am chewing.
I think our tablemate is referring to the electoral race at first
before I understand my error. This one is tough—its nacreous, butterfly
shell swings shut on its hinges, small black wings locked like a mouth.
The others at the table are expectant as though we're about to share a
secret. The mussel lodges between my teeth. A toothpick would be
handy. I should have ordered soup.

Sometimes white women tell me they find him—my husband—
attractive. Sometimes I smile. Sometimes I don't.
Prying things open takes effort and sometimes I'm too tired to do it.
Sometimes I think about the ball and chain dragging along behind
the dangerous feminine. But tonight I eat steamed mussels swimming
in wine and tarragon. We're all filter feeders of some kind or another.
It's the only way to survive.

When you were younger, single, you were mistaken
for the black man the police were looking for—who, apparently,
could have been your twin. You were hauled in for questioning
but then, like the fish in the nursery rhyme, they let you go again.

How easy it would have been for them to keep you.
I duel with another mussel, try to be civilized. My black
husband was permitted to mature out in the open. My black
father, on the other hand, died at fifty-one. The English doctor
broke the news to my mother saying she was better off
without him — my mother being an attractive young white woman
in 1961. I reach for another mussel. It clings to its shell like something
                                                                    livid.
I jab it with a fork and twist hard. It will not detach itself.
Our tablemate is saying she likes Obama. Finds him attractive,
articulate. But why, she asks us, is he so…so…

Obama, son of Abraham, cuff-linked to a house as white as Snow
                                                        White,
when will the wistful weltering world stop expecting you
to croon it back to sleep?

5 South 43rd Street, Floor 2

Yolanda Wisher

Sometimes we would get hungry for the neighborhood.
Walk up the sidewalk towards Chestnut Street.
Speak to the Rev holding the light-skinned baby,
ask his son to come put a new inner tube on my bike.
Cross Ludlow, past the mailbox on the corner,
Risqué Video, Dino's Pizza, and the Emerald Laundromat.
The fruit trucks tucked into 44th Street on the left,
house eyes shut with boards, fringes of children.
Once we went into a store sunk into the street,
owned by a Cambodian woman. She sold everything,
from evening gowns to soup. Over to Walnut and 45th,
where the Muslim cat sells this chicken wrapped in pita,
draped in cucumber sauce. The pregnant woman
behind the counter writes our order out in Arabic.
We grab a juice from the freezer, some chips,
eye the bean and sweet potato pies.

Back into the hot breath of West Philly, sun is setting.
The sky is smeared squash, tangerines in a glaze.
Three girls and one boy jump doubledutch. A white man
hustles from the video store with a black plastic bag.
We look for money in the street, steal flowers
from the church lawn. The shit stain from the wino
is still on our step. Mr. Jim is washing a car for cash.

John is cleaning his rims to Buju Banton.
Noel is talking sweetly to the big blue-eyed woman.
Linda, on her way to the restaurant. The sister
in the wheelchair buzzes by with her headphones on.

One night, a man was shot and killed on this block,
right outside our thick wood door. But not today.
Today is one of those days to come home from walking
in the world, leave the windows open, start a pot of
black beans. Smoke some Alice Coltrane. Cut up
some fruit, toenails. Hold on to the moment
as if time is taking your blood pressure.

Unrest in Baton Rouge

Tracy K. Smith

after the photo by Jonathan Bachman

Our bodies run with ink dark blood.
Blood pools in the pavement's seams.

Is it strange to say love is a language
Few practice, but all, or near all speak?

Even the men in black armor, the ones
Jangling handcuffs and keys, what else

Are they so buffered against, if not love's blade
Sizing up the heart's familiar meat?

We watch and grieve. We sleep, stir, eat.
Love: the heart sliced open, gutted, clean.

Love: naked almost in the everlasting street,
Skirt lifted by a different kind of breeze.

Quare

L. Lamar Wilson

A man is a woman inside
Waiting to come home.
A man inside a woman is
A mother-of-pearl, a wading
Handmaiden, inside a man
Made prison, prism of light.
At the end of that tunnel: new birth.
New berth? Tunnel to that end,
Light the prism, prison-break
Everyman's woe. Inside
Every man lies   The seed of
Mother's tears   petaled, pearled.
Seven weeks whole. Wonderfully
She. Made us a beauty. Inside. Ascend.
Ussin. Us/sin. Us>sin. Us>skin.
Us skin & sin less & iridescent.
All spirit, no shade, no shame.
Liminal. Limn it all. One nation
Undone. God<less. Now what?
O Amma, may I eye inside
The we *we* was! Decode the cipher
We forgot: *To Whom It May Concern,*
Keep This Nigger-Boy Running. O
woe Man-cum-woman hater,

O nacre, O negus — never nigger —
Cry out & She will rise. Inside us.
She's waiting, Black (wo)man
Stop running. Come home.

after E. Patrick Johnson, Sharon P. Holland,
& Ralph Waldo Ellison

Some Young Kings

Roger Reeves

The Mike Tyson in me sings like a narwhal
minus the nasally twang of sleeping in a cold ocean,
the unsightly barnacles latched to the mattress
of skin just below my eye, the white horn
jutting out from the top of my head —
oh god bless us mutts — the basset-blood-
hound mulattoes, the pug-mixed puppies
left behind the dog pound's cinder-block walls
as German Shepherds, Labradoodles,
and Portuguese Water-Dogs turn their inbred behinds
and narrow backs at our small-mouthed blues.
It's hard to smile with an ear in your mouth,
two names, and a daughter hanging by the thread
from the railing of a treadmill. Oh neck
and North Carolina and a white coat of paint
for all the faces of my negro friends
hanging from trees in Salisbury.
Greensboro. And Guilford County.
The hummingbirds inside my chest,
with their needle-nosed pliers for tongues
and hammer-heavy wings, have left a mess
of ticks in my lungs and a punctured lullaby
in my throat. Little boy blue come blow
your horn. The cow's in the meadow.

And Dorothy's alone in the corn with Jack,

his black fingers, the brass of his lips,

the half-moons of his fingernails clicking

along her legs until she howls—

Charlie Parker. Charlie Parker. Charlie Parker.

Oz is a man with a mute body

on an HBO original show that I am too afraid to watch

for fear of finding my uncle,

or a man that looks like my uncle,

which means finding a man that looks like me

in another man's embrace or slumped over a shiv

made from a mattress coil and a bar of Ivory soap.

Most young kings return home without their heads.

It's 1941, and Jack Johnson still loves white women,

and my mother won't forgive him.

If she can't use your comb, don't bring her home,

my mother says in 1998. It's 2009,

and I still love white women.

Charlie Parker. Charlie Parker. Charlie Parker.

Often, I click the heels of my Nikes together

when talking to the police, I am a cricket

crushed beneath a car's balding black tires.

Most young kings return home without their heads.

We Are Not Responsible

Harryette Mullen

We are not responsible for your lost or stolen relatives.
We cannot guarantee your safety if you disobey our instructions.
We do not endorse the causes or claims of people begging for handouts.
We reserve the right to refuse service to anyone.

Your ticket does not guarantee that we will honor your reservations.
In order to facilitate our procedures, please limit your carrying on.
Before taking off, please extinguish all smoldering resentments.

If you cannot understand English, you will be moved out of the way.
In the event of a loss, you'd better look out for yourself.
Your insurance was cancelled because we can no longer handle
your frightful claims. Our handlers lost your luggage and we
are unable to find the key to your legal case.

You were detained for interrogation because you fit the profile.
You are not presumed to be innocent if the police
have reason to suspect you are carrying a concealed wallet.
It's not our fault you were born wearing a gang color.
It is not our obligation to inform you of your rights.

Step aside, please, while our officer inspects your bad attitude.

You have no rights we are bound to respect.

Please remain calm, or we can't be held responsible

for what happens to you.

Carl's Barbershop

The peppermint stripes spinning

The shaving cream

The crowding around the TV

The razor

The photo of Malcolm X and Dr. King

The Coca Cola machine

That still accepts dimes

The radio playing the Oldies

The trash talking

The "nobody can touch Otis Redding

& that's a fact jack"

The bullet hole

The empty chair

The fades

The rust colored tile

The high tops

The baby photos

The pointing, that's my little girl when she was a baby

The neighborhood—everything—changing

The slopes, The fro-hawks, the hieroglyphs

The scissors slicing the air

The fragrant coconut afro sheen

that makes you choke each time

(You never complain)

The parts

The small rectangular handheld mirror

The vanity, The one-two look & vogue

The folded twenty plus five

The handshake

The pause—

On Being Called the N-Word in Atlanta, 2016: A Southern Ghazal

teri elam

At six, barely knowing her A-B-Cs, first time this Southern girl called
nigger
On the playground, hollow-pointed-word shot: her pint-sized heart
caught "nigger"

Before flawless, now skewered, her heated veins drain their first
blues — shame
By *Run Spot Run* in school, kids learn mean tricks & invisible-ink her,
nigger

At recess, taunting "eeny-meeny miney moe" boys run behind to snatch
her up
When "it" in hide-n-seek, but she knows she "ain't nobody's hollering
nigger"

Her mama, who fought their fire with her own, would say, then roil
ablaze after
Soiled-cotton-mouths snuff-drawled & spat at them both, "goddamn
niggers"

Now older than her mother then, her toughened-tongue tries remixing to untooth it
But Southern teeth grow fangs, this time a more forceful bite, "you nigger-bitch"

And as if stuck in place, age six, she hemorrhages & rages & this Southern girl,
Boils & chokes up when venomous tongues noose-tie her name, call me — nigger.

The President Has Never Said the Word *Black*

Morgan Parker

To the extent that one begins
to wonder if he is broken.

It is not so difficult to open
teeth and brass taxes.

The president is all like
five on the bleep hand side.

The president be like
we lost a young   boy today.

The pursuit of happiness
is guaranteed for all fellow   Americans.

He is nobody special like us.
He says brothers and sisters.

What kind of bodies are movable
and feasts. What color are visions.

When he opens his mouth
a chameleon is inside, starving.

[this to say i am more terrified of capitalism than any wildlife encounter]

Jasmine Elizabeth Smith

that it was never natural to climb mountains
unless in flight.
that my body was held accountable
not by asylum of land
that called me near
perfect as trilliums and blanket-flowers.
that i am not made of metal
nor mountaineer's ice-pick—
& even the glacier-fed cliff swallows who roost daylight-reeves must rest
to dream whereabouts of southern-bound stars. that if they are counted
am i too safe enough to pause—
to spit up mouthfuls of gravel in thirst, or gather
myself phlox, balsam root? these my own kind service in absence of
summit.

In the Event Of

Shane McCrae

Officer how you know I'm dancing is the body
-cam. Look, I'm riding centuries of whips, the first half

Of the ghost, arms out the window up, the second half
Arms flat on the pavement, palms down, now the ghost is whole

My arms stretched forward, like I'm bowing, but if I
Were standing, stretched above my head. Officer how

You know I'm dead is that I seem to bow to you

Happy

Kevin Powell

I
would
be
forever
happy
if
I
could
be
that
yellow-eyed
black
bird
finally
released
from
its
cage
and
able
to
soar
freely
into

the

purple sky

any

purple sky

like

I

own it

without

any

worry

or

fear

that

someone

anyone

would try

to

harm

me

just

because

of

how

I

fly

or

the

color

288

of

my

wings

Thursday, June 4, 2020

6:41 a.m.

Holla

Evie Shockley

i don't know what's after
death, but i do know my
ancestors. and if what comes next
wasn't better than *this*
mess, we'd have heard about it. there'd
be some half-embodied, half-
spectral stank attitude
up in the kitchen or on the front
stoop, and wouldn't nobody
get no rest, let alone peace. if what
comes next didn't outstrip
this world for beauty, there'd be
some gangster grievances
to deal with. you think not
harriet tubman nor tupac shakur
would have something to say?
you figure neither ella fitzgerald
nor ella baker would sound
off? do you really believe
that malcolm wouldn't have the means
necessary to let folks know
if he found things unacceptable
at the other end of his transition?
we'd be minding our own business,

and suddenly

a voice carrying 30-odd years of *hell-no*

and 3 continents of *you-gots-to-be-*

kidding-me would be all *SING, MUSE,*

OF THE WRATH OF A PHILLIS, pentameting

all over your i-ams. young emmett

would turn up everywhere we look,

kicked back and whistling *dixie*

from under that cocked fedora

in a very minor key. we'd have ida b. wells

and june jordan reporting

on the universe's dirty drawers, leaving no

question unasked and no record

unread. mlk would give book,

chapter, and verse on the meaning of *promised*

land. du bois would loosen his cravat,

morrison would release her death stare,

and you'd *know* it was on. look,

i don't have the goods

on what comes after death. another pass

at a planet that's still more forest

than concrete? a voyage

into dark matter with a chance

to send our atoms back

as rainfall or baby's breath? a party

hosted on the soular plane

by duke ellington, prince, and ntozake

shange? maybe a front-row seat

for viewing the human animal
finally getting ready to evolve? hey,
someday we'll all get
the dirt. but rest assured, if it wasn't better
than *this* ish, i'd have already gotten
word.

WHEN I SEE THE STARS: PRAISE POEMS

A Prayer for Workers

Yusef Komunyakaa

Bless the woman, man, & child
   who honor Earth by opening shine
in the soil—the splayed hour
   between dampness & dust—to plant
a few seedlings in furrows, & then pray
   for cooling rain. Bless the fields,
the catch, the hunt, & the wild fruit,
   & let no one go hungry tonight
or tomorrow. Let the wind & birds
   seed a future ferried into villages
& towns the other side of mountains
   along nameless rivers. Bless those
born with hands made to do work,
   hewn timbers & stone raised from earth
& shaped in circles, who know the geometry
   of corners, & please level the foundation
& pitch a roof so good work isn't diminished
   by rain. Bless the farmer with clouds
in his head, who lugs baskets of dung
   so termites can carve their hives
that hold water long after a downpour
   has gone across the desert & seeds
sprout into a contiguous greening.
   Bless the iridescent beetle working

to haul the heavens down, to journey
    from moon dust to excrement.
The wage-slave's two steps from Dickens's
    tenements among a den of thieves,
blind soothsayers who know shambles
    where migrants feathered the nests
of straw bosses as the stonecutters
    perfect profiles of robber barons
in granite & marble in town squares
    along highways paved for Hollywood.
Bless souls laboring in sweatshops,
    & each calabash dipper of water,
the major & minor litanies & ganglia
    dangling from promises at the mouth
of the cave, the catcher of vipers at dawn
    in the canebrake & flowering fields,
not for the love of money but for bread
    & clabber on a thick gray slab table,
for the simple blessings in a small town
    of the storytellers drunk on grog.
Bless the cobbler, molding leather
    on his steel latch, kneading softness
& give into a red shoe & a work boot,
    never giving more to one than the other,
& also the weaver with closed eyes,
    whose fingers play the loops & ties,
as if nothing else matters, daybreak
    to sunset, as stories of a people

grow into an epic stitched down
   through the ages, the outsider artists,
going from twine & hue, cut & tag,
   an ironmonger's credo of steam rising from buckets
of water & metal dust, & the clang
   of a hammer against an anvil,
& the ragtag ones, the motley crew
   at the end of the line, singing ballads
& keeping time on a battered tin drum.

Heaven: For Nikki Giovanni's 80th Birthday

Renée Watson

"Heaven must be a mess. All those Black women up there
bragging about their children."—Nikki Giovanni

Every year on the seventh of June
heaven throws a birthday party

for Nikki.

Coretta is there. She's protective of Aiyana and Hadiya.
She introduces them to Sandra and Breonna, keeps them close.
And surely Harriet and Fannie and Rosa are swapping stories of how
they got over.
And Lucille and Gwendolyn and Margaret recite sonnets, teach them to
　　Betty.
And Toni and Maya are writing jubilees for the angels to sing.
And you better believe Whitney is showing out
and Nina and Aretha and Mahalia, too.
And no doubt there are women there whose names we don't know:
grandmas and mommas and aunties and sisters and cousins
and best friends and used to be friends and strangers

and my momma, Carrie Elizabeth, she is there, too.

And they do what Black women always do when we gather.
Feast and gossip and fill time with laughter and reminiscing.

And they say what Black women always say when we talk with God.
Thank Him for what He's done, plead with Him to go easy on us, ask Him,
Haven't Black women suffered enough?

And before the feast ends, Nikki's grandmother takes my mother by her
hand,
walks her to the corner of the sky, says, *Look at our babies, see them
down there?*
Ain't they a wonder?

And all the Black women in heaven sing to the poet Nikki,
whose name means victorious, whose name ushers in
revolution and radical love.

And all the Black women in heaven testify and thank God
for Nikki, the truth-teller, for Nikki, the nurturer,
for Nikki, the lover of chocolate & Knoxville & Ohio & Tupac & jazz
& gospel

& Black folks

Oh, how she loves us, they sing. *Oh, how she shows us love.*

And if you listen close, you can hear their voices echoing from Heaven
in the shifting wind,

in the sprinkle from clouds, in the whisper of a sinking sun, in the
shimmering stars,
in the crashing waves, in the first bloom of flower:

Oh, how we love you, Nikki, they sing. *Oh, Nikki, how you are loved.*
Oh, Nikki, thank you for loving us. Oh, Nikki, thank you for showing us
how to love.
Oh, Nikki, thank you for teaching us "Black love is Black wealth."
Oh, Nikki, thank you for showing us how.

Oh, Nikki, thank you, thank you.

The Origins of the Artist: Natalie Cole

Toi Derricotte

My father
was black, black

as suede,
black as the ace

of spades, black
as the grave. Black

humbled him
and made him

proud. At first
there was a space

between us,
a mirror flashed

back at me. Then
his blackness

entered
me like God.

Elegy for Chadwick Boseman

Len Lawson

The Black Panther lives forever
His mantle passes from generation to generation
But this, this was a man
Flesh and bone breathing among us
Living, smiling, crossing his arms at his chest
For us, for all of us with melanin souls
For the spirits in our black chests
Our Ambassador of Blackness
When our own country allows our genocide
When our protectors keep blasting
Our bodies into the ancestral plane
A hero who gave us black icons on screen
Instead of black blood canvasing pavement
Lambs dragged to brazen altars at traffic stops
We beheld his CGI glory descending in *Endgame*
Second coming from a morning star portal
With every African regality, ancestor, and deity
Filling his chest and healing arms with valor
We salute
Fists raised
Eyes lifted
Hearts heavy with vibranium

When I See the Stars in the Night Sky

Joy Priest

I think of Whitney Houston   in her sequined glamour
    She's centerstage   It's 1988   Her head
        Thrown back against a black backdrop   She is the only thing
    glowing   So distant   from us in the universe

    of her voice   She is already dying   when
I hear her sing the first time   When I slip inside
    my rhinestone leotard white tights   Before a mic
        My vocal chords are still elastic   Vibrating harpstring

    Not yet sclerotic with unlovely smoke   and shame
    I'm drawn to Whitney like a cardinal on a branch
in winter   Beauty too bright for camouflage   Her story

a constellation twinned with mine. I love myself because of her. Our
sweet lip sweat sparkling in the flame
light. I went home inside myself too. The world became so small. Secrets
collapsing my life into a vacuum.
To burn a little longer—Whitney, you know   no one is coming—
you must   save yourself.

Hip Hop Analogies

Tara Betts

after Miguel and Erykah Badu

If you be the needle,

    I be the LP.

If you be the buffed wall,

    I be the Krylon.

If you be the backspin,

    I be the break.

If you be the head nod,

    I be the bass line.

If you be a Phillie,

    I be the razor.

If you be the microphone,

    then I be the palm.

If you be the cipher,

    then I be the beatbox.

If you be hands thrown up,

    then I be yes, yes, y'all.

If you be throwback,

    then I be remix.

If you be footwork,

    then I be uprock.

If you be turntable,

    then I be crossfader.

If you be downtown C train,

    then I be southbound Red Line.

If you be shell toes,

    then I be hoodie.

If you be freestyle,

    then I be piece book.

If you be Sharpie,

    then I be tag.

If you be boy,

    then I be girl

    who wants to

    sync samples

    into classic.

For ben harper (7:42pm 1-18-02)

Jessica Care Moore

There are gardens on mercury who
Water themselves in praise of your
Guitar strings

There are newborn babies born quietly
In the middle of the night
Who secretly cry in key
To honor your voice

There are sculptors who revel
As chiseled native cheekbones
Rest easily
Inside the statue of your
Face

There are poets who lay down pens
Light candles, drink heavily and meditate
Waiting for a new metaphor to present itself
Inside the blurry moment
When everything goes black
And inspiration
dizzily arrives
struggle leaves
and your music begins

For a moment, you were there.

Strumming the ancestors blues
Pickin' and praying to elders
Calling out to the prophets before u
Telling on the goddess as she prepares
To bottle the wind for the coyotes who
Want to sweep her off her feet

She hears you singing through indifference
She hears you filling up the wounds of the soulless

We wear the crown of thorns
We write for the believers in the earth
There are traveling spirits who knew your birth name
Whispering in your childhood ear
When you were first in search of sound
For a moment. I was there

Watching oppression be set into the fire
The chosen people dancing and sweating and living
The love they always had but couldn't find
Scatting& yodeling & sliding
Across the wire and between your fingers
Rising with the intention of the sun
you sung...

Angels stopped to test their wings

Witnessing this brown black man in flight
A thousand miles an hour
Without leaving the chair
or microphone
channeling acoustic stories from somebody's
great grand-mammas breasts

I wrote this poem
In honor of the violet, rose and gypsy flowers
Who remember we breathe inside the soil
I wrote this poem for lovers who's hearts
Have stopped believing in
fortunate accidents

I wrote this poem for artists who
Still create with purpose & truth
Poets who make ugly
The most beautiful thing in the world

I wrote this in honor of you
Because you let me read my poem
When I was just beginning my journey
And for that too
I will always remember you.

My Poems

Joanna Crowell

He asks,
"What do you do with your poems?"

I reply:

I play with them. I fight with them. I flirt with
them. I avert from them. I dress up for them. I am
stripped down by them. I skinny dip into them. I
dance naked on them. Yeah, I even get jiggy wit'
em! I sing the blues out of them. I pour the joy
back into them. I open my French doors for them.
I abstain from them. I get wet waiting for them.
I am a drunken fool for them. I take twelve steps
toward them. I am sobered by them.

I carve them. I chip away at them. I get into the
grooves of them. I smooth my surfaces with them.
I accept my flaws because of them. I am flattered
by them. I am humbled in them. I am beautiful.
To them.

I stop to smell the roses with them. I notice every
detail in them. I pick them. I am pricked by them.
I bleed with them. I die in them. I ascend to

them. I am reborn through them. I birth them.

I hold hands with them. I face my fear with
them. I tremble in them. I share my secrets with
them. I share my secrets with the world through
them. I cry for the world on them. My tears are
caught by them. I am baptized by them. I drown
in them. I float above them. I am consoled by
them. I find my soul in them. I am emboldened
by them. I am subtle in them. I cuddle with them.
I like to spoon with them. I become consumed by
them. I taste every vowel of them. I swallow the
sum of them. I drink every consonant of them. I
am quenched by them.

I breathe them. I live them.

I am them.

And then

    I give them away.

Aubade to Langston

Rachel Eliza Griffiths

When the light wakes & finds again
the music of brooms in Mexico,
when daylight pulls our hands from grief,
& hearts cleaned raw with sawdust
& saltwater flood their dazzling vessels,
when the catfish in the river
raise their eyelids towards your face,
when sweetgrass bends in waves
across battlefields where sweat
& sugar marry, when we hear our people
wearing tongues fine with plain
greeting: How You Doing, Good Morning
when I pour coffee & remember
my mother's love of buttered grits,
when the trains far away in memory
begin to turn their engines toward
a deep past of knowing,
when all I want to do is burn
my masks, when I see a woman
walking down the street holding her mind
like a leather belt, when I pluck a blues note
for my lazy shadow & cast its soul from my page,
when I see God's eyes looking up at black folks
flying between moonlight & museum,

when I see a good-looking people
who are my truest poetry,
when I pick up this pencil like a flute
& blow myself away from my death,
I listen to you again beneath the mercy
of a blue morning's grammar.

What Women Are Made Of

Bianca Lynne Spriggs

There are many kinds of open.
—Audre Lorde

We are all ventricle, spine, lung, larynx, and gut.
Clavicle and nape, what lies forked in an open palm;

we are follicle and temple. We are ankle, arch,
sole. Pore and rib, pelvis and root

and tongue. We are wishbone and gland and molar
and lobe. We are hippocampus and exposed nerve

and cornea. Areola, pigment, melanin, and nails.
Varicose. Cellulite. Divining rod. Sinew and tissue,

saliva and silt. We are blood and salt, clay and aquifer.
We are breath and flame and stratosphere. Palimpsest

and bibelot and cloisonné fine lines. Marigold, hydrangea,
and dimple. Nightlight, satellite, and stubble. We are

pinnacle, plummet, dark circles, and dark matter.
A constellation of freckles and specters and miracles

and lashes. Both bent and erect, we are all give
and give back. We are volta and girder. Make an incision

in our nectary and Painted Ladies sail forth, riding the back
of a warm wind, plumed with love and things like love.

Crack us down to the marrow, and you may find us full
of cicada husks and sand dollars and salted maple taffy

weary of welding together our daydreams. All sweet tea,
razor blades, carbon, and patchwork quilts of Good God!

and *Lord have mercy!* Our hands remember how to turn
the earth before we do. Our intestinal fortitude? Cumulonimbus

streaked with saffron light. Our foundation? Not in our limbs
or hips; this comes first as an amen, a hallelujah, a suckling,

swaddled psalm sung at the cosmos's breast. You want to
know what women are made of? Open wide and find out.

ruth (for a sister poet)

Michael Datcher

she speaks

winds whirl

honeysuckle and jasmine meet

to ponder

why the air is sweeter

now

amber hues swirl

blue and bluest

before they jump black

then ease back into rustic amber

as the last words

the lucky ones

(they knew her longer)

leave her lips

slowly

a spurned sycamore

leans goodbye

while its lone leaf

willingly leaps to death

crooning

"just to be close to you girl"

the four winds sing background

while escorting the spiraling

lovelorn

to the nape

beneath her ear

it rustles her name

before falling to the grass

ruthless

and dead

next to her last words

(the lucky ones)

forever

Black Gold Redux (for Nina Simone)

Jacqueline Johnson

Vocalized anger of a generation
lived in your throat.
Sometimes you left yourself
   while still at the piano.

Cultivated respect for sound making,
form of the body.
Demanded the best,
   did not always receive it.

Wore golden garments of adornment:
wrist size earrings, raw silk afro.
Made your musicians either keep up or
get off the stage.

Didn't really need a drum
your voice was chant,
   sea island moan,
      a priestess prayer song.

for duke ellington

Reuben Jackson

music is your mistress;
demanding constant love
and international settings.

as always, you stroll beside her.

again, grumpy orchestra
springs into elegance at the drop
of your hand

even so, there are casualties.

the years pass
you bury rabbit and swee'pea,
run your fingers across the black keys,
dip the color into your hair

cancerous nodes
rush toward a harrowing cadenza,
pen kisses paper,

a lover
in no particular hurry,
the music reveals itself
a negligee black note at a time.

Don't Let Me Be Lonely [Mahalia Jackson is a genius.]

Claudia Rankine

Mahalia Jackson is a genius. Or Mahalia Jackson has genius. The man I am with is trying to make a distinction. I am uncomfortable with his need to make this distinction because his inquiry begins to approach subtle shades of racism, classism, or sexism. It is hard to know which. Mahalia Jackson never finished the eighth grade, or Mahalia's genius is based on the collision of her voice with her spirituality. True spirituality is its own force. I am not sure how to respond to all this. I change the subject instead.

We have just seen George Wein's documentary, *Louis Armstrong at Newport, 1971*. In the auditorium a room full of strangers listened to Mahalia Jackson sing "Let There Be Peace on Earth" and stood up and gave a standing ovation to a movie screen. Her clarity of vision crosses thirty years to address intimately each of us. It is as if her voice has always been dormant within us, waiting to be awakened, even though "it had to go through its own lack of answers, through terrifying silence, (and) through the thousand darknesses of murderous speech."

Perhaps Mahalia, like Paul Celan, has already lived all our lives for us. Perhaps that is the definition of genius. Hegel says, "Each man hopes and believes he is better than the world which is his, but the man who is better merely expresses this same world better than the others." Mahalia Jackson sings as if it is the last thing she intends to do. And even though the lyrics of the song are, "Let there be peace on earth and let it begin with me," I am hearing, *Let it begin in me.*

For John Lewis, who loved to dance

Pearl Cleage

He loved to dance, my fearless friend.

He also loved to sing.

Freedom songs. Love songs. Motown songs. Spirit songs.

Because even in a war, he knew there was dancing in the street

And laughter in the sweet way he loved to dance.

My fearless, peerless friend,

Who knew that even in a war

There is joy that comes in the morning

And stays all night.

There is hope that comes at sunrise

And stays to meet the moon

And not a moment too soon

To give the music one more chance

To know the power of our warrior's stance

Our warrior's dance

To know that he is dancing still

In my dreams

He is dancing still.

Soul Train

Allison Joseph

Oh how I wanted to be a dancer
those Saturday mornings in the
living room, neglecting chores

to gape at the whirling people
on our television: the shapely
and self-knowing brownskinned

women who dared stare straight
at the camera, the men strong,
athletically gifted as they

leaped, landed in full splits.
No black people I knew lived
like this—dressed in sequins,

makeup, men's hair slicked
back like 40s gangsters,
women in skin-tight, merciless

spandex, daring heels higher
than I could imagine walking in,
much less dancing. And that

dancing!—full of sex, swagger,
life—a communal rite where
everyone arched, swayed, shimmered

and shimmied, hands overhead
in celebration, bodies moving
to their own influences, lithe

under music pumping from studio
speakers, beneath the neon letters
that spelled out SOUL TRAIN—

the hippest trip in America.
I'd try to dance, to keep up,
moving like the figures on

the screen, hoping the rhythm
could hit me in that same
hard way, that same mission

of shake and groove, leaving
my dust rag behind, ignoring
the furniture and the polish

to step and turn as they did,
my approximation nowhere near
as clever or seductive, faking

it as best I knew how, shaking
my 12 year old self as if something
deep depended upon the right move,

the righteous step, the insistent
groove I followed, yearning to get
it right, to move like those dancers—

blessed by funk, touched with rhythm,
confident in their motions, clothes,
their spinning and experienced bodies.

for allison joseph
kwansaba

Van G. Garrett

the pretty-brown marble-colored-eyed poet
who pounced on donya and felt badly
found ways to front-pocket the bronx
writing beyond mount olympus — hair — race — barbie
a mess of yams and pigeon peas
with music — and forms — and penned elegies
bundled like crabs and midwest orchard trees

I, Master (For David Drake, Enslaved Potter-Poet)

Glenis Redmond

Who drives de whip
be at de helm *Work harder, boy,*

don't nobody have tell me,
back into dis clay I shoulder dis grind.

See my pots and you'll know Ise yoked
not by lash, but by every chamber of my heart.

What my mouth don't say my hands do
my pots be what most people ain't: whole

Head down Ise lifted up higher than the one
tryin his best to beat me down

Into each mound I pull a body into being
with dese hands burns a fire dat can't be put out

Sometimes I get puffed upwild turkey like
I do my best to smooth my feathers down

bend my self around prayer Here I stand
closes to de Lawd, my one true master.

He turns de world, I spin dis wheel
as I breathe life into these lumps—

I too from mud make miracles.

San Diego and Matisse

Clarence Major

1. INSIDE FROM THE PERSPECTIVE OF A TREE

Beautiful women in smoky blue culottes
lying around on fluffy pink pillows
beneath windows onto charming views,
sea views, seasonal leaves and trees.
Inside is outside and outside inside.
Smell of saltwater swimming in the room.

2. OUTSIDE FROM THE PERSPECTIVE OF A ROCKING
   CHAIR

Shadow of lighthouse along the beach.
Whales spotted every day lately
though winter's two months yet.
The evening is as warm as an interior.
Silverlight lagoonlight, snorkeling light.
And a line of joggers against last light.
Blue smoke snaking up the pink sky.

Ashe

Kevin Young

For years I've wanted to write
    how exactly I felt
with you hovering

    on my wall, framed, mid-
air, about to strike
    the ball above you,

Arthur Ashe—in your tennis whites
    I pictured you lifted
into whatever came after

    this photo's instant—firing
a volley, or striking a serve
    down the throat

of your opponent
    like a pill.
Your signature

    below my name
seemed more real to me
    than most things—bullies,

or whatever wisdom got cracked
　　out of me like a knuckle—
more real than being

　　unable to see without glass
before my eyes. I saw you
　　sported glasses too.

Your hair a microphone cover
　　to help keep
the static down. Even

　　your photo has a sound—
call it *About to be.*
　　Call it *Maybe*—

no, *Probably*—
　　name it
after every unlikely

you made into something.
　　You swing
in my head like Count Basie

　　only there's no
royalty, no music anymore
　　like yours.

Queen Bess

Kimberly A. Collins

Do you know you have never lived until you have flown?
——*Bessie Coleman*

A shooting star singing through sky
An unfettered falcon without fear of flight
Flapping wings against a Texas one-room shack
Bessie couldn't jot down *her* Chicago bound blues

An unfettered falcon without fear of flight
She came perched between clouds daring sons
Bessie couldn't jot down *her* Chicago bound blues
She *be runnin' dem browns down*

She came perched between clouds daring sons
Swallowing men whole, spitting them out to fly
She be *runnin' dem browns down*
Swallowing her wind, she steals their laughter

Swallowing men whole, she spits them out to fly
She wants her men phoenix-like   lighting skies
Swallowing her wind, she steals their laughter
Hail Queen Bess! She claims her throne

She wants her men phoenix-like   lighting skies

She needs to walk before she flies

Hail Queen Bess! She claims her throne

Barren beds mourn her departure

She needs to walk before she flies

Twirling through rainbows

Barren beds mourn her departure

She teaches Nina to sing "Mississippi Goddam"!

Twirling through rainbows

Without Jim Crow, up there, everyone is free

She teaches Nina to sing "Mississippi Goddam"!

Prepares Odetta's crown continuing freedom's fight

Without Jim Crow, up there, everyone is free

She is France's First Lady Liberty   chasing wind

She prepares Odetta's crown continuing freedom's fight

She came singing about planes and being black and flying

She is France's First Lady Liberty   chasing wind

Her gut speaks about flying to feel alive

She came singing about planes and being black and flying

A shooting star singing through sky

The Ragged and the Beautiful

Safiya Sinclair

Doubt is a storming bull, crashing through
the blue-wide windows of myself. Here in the heart
of my heart where it never stops raining,

I am an outsider looking in. But in the garden
of my good days, no body is wrong. Here every
flower grows ragged and sideways and always

beautiful. We bloom with the outcasts,
our soon-to-be sunlit, we dreamers. We are strange
and unbelonging. Yes. We are just enough

of ourselves to catch the wind in our feathers,
and fly so perfectly away.

brown-eyed girls

Gerald L. Coleman

(for every one of you)

brown-eyed
girls
make the world
go round
like the corner
piece
of a pan of brownies
a sleeve
of girl scout
cookies
or the law
of conservation
of energy
comforting me
that joy cannot
be destroyed
it simply changes
form

brown-haired girls
make
the sun shine

like
hopping in puddles
ice cream on
noses
or getting shit done
mending
the world
and making it
safe
for brown skin
boys

we don't
bring out
the confetti
the bright lights
the stars
in our eyes
for
brown-eyed girls
even when
they are kindly
completely
saving
the world

Zebra (For My Son)

You are not who they say you are.
You are Nubian with white stripes

and sport a Mohawk for a mane.
Once hunted to extinction,

your deafening bray is a song for the fallen.
Some might even say you are God's mistake.

But how ordinary the world would be without you.
They will say stay in your herd, stick close to your mother's side.

Remember, you are all equine.
Put another way, you are a wild ass.

Raise those ears. Kick your legs.
Gaze that impenetrable stare.

Your forefathers once grazed on African grasses.
Your place in this world is the one you claim.

Quality: Gwendolyn Brooks at 73

Haki R. Madhubuti

June 7, 1990

breath,
life after seven decades plus three years
is a lot of breathing. seventy three years on this
earth is a lot of taking in and giving out, is a
life of coming from somewhere and for many a bunch
of going nowhere.

how do we celebrate a poet who has created
music with words for over fifty years, who has
showered magic on her people, who has redefined
poetry into a black world exactness
thereby giving the universe an insight into
darkroads?

just say she interprets beauty and wants to
give life, say she is patient with phoniness
and doesn't mind people calling her gwen or sister.
say she sees the genius in our children, is visionary
about possibilities, sees as clearly as ray charles and
stevie wonder, hears like determined elephants looking
for food. say that her touch is fine wood, her memory
is like an african roadmap detailing adventure and

clarity, yet returning to chicago's south evans
to record the journey. say her voice is majestic
and magnetic as she speaks in poetry, rhythms, song
and spirited trumpets, say she is dark skinned,
melanin rich, small-boned, hurricane-willed,
with a mind like a tornado redefining the landscape.

life after seven decades plus three years
is a lot of breathing.
gwendolyn, gwen, sister g has
not disappointed our expectations.
in the middle
of her eldership she brings us
vigorous language, memory,
illumination.

she brings breath.

A Love Poem Written for Sterling Brown

Sonia Sanchez

(after reading a New York Times *article re
a mummy kept preserved for about 300 years)*

I'm gonna get me some mummy tape for your love
preserve it for 3000 years or more
I'm gonna let the world see you
tapping a blue shell dance of love
I'm gonna ride your love bareback
on totem poles
bear your image on mountains
turning in ocean sleep
string your sighs thru the rainbow
of old age.
In the midst of desert people and times
I'm gonna fly your red/eagle/laughter 'cross the sky.

Whispers on the Wave

Tonya Maria Matthews

whispers on the wave say *daughter*
when I asked God why take me through such troubled water
He said your enemies can't swim

connections in the dirt
mirror our skin
whispers on the wave say *daughter*

connections in the drum
order our step
whispers on the wave say *daughter*

a man in yoke benefits nothing
a woman enchained by waist by wrist by ankle is never grateful
a child with a story on the heart
is never forgetful

banned books never stop the telling
bound feet never stop the running
bedazzled revision never outshines the truth
a child with a story on the heart
is a child that knows her own name

what happens to that dream deferred?

it boils blood like indigo
shakes soul like rice
salts tongue like ocean
then in simple rebellious motion
reinvents itself as feathered beast
to go back and fetch everything
ancestors riding on the left wing
descendants on the right

our people's bones became stepping stones
and so now we walk on water

and now you reckoning with a daughter
who knows the story

Who is the story

We be the story

We claim the story

We heal
We shield
We build
We bold
We hold
and we always told the story

I am still here
through the tale of all tales
my history the holiest of grails

and this lioness shall be historian
connected through the dirt
connected through the drum
anchored in our story
protected through troubled water
whispers on the wave say

daughter

Praise

Angelo Geter

Today I will praise.
I will praise the sun
For showering its light
On this darkened vessel.
I will praise its shine.
Praise the way it wraps
My skin in ultraviolet ultimatums
Demanding to be seen.
I will lift my hands in adoration
Of how something so bright
Could be so heavy.
I will praise the ground
That did not make feast of these bones.
Praise the casket
That did not become a shelter for flesh.
Praise the bullets
That called in sick to work.
Praise the trigger
That went on vacation.
Praise the chalk
That did not outline a body today.
Praise the body
For still being a body
And not a headstone.
Praise the body,

For being a body and not a police report

Praise the body

For being a body and not a memory

No one wants to forget.

Praise the memories.

Praise the laughs and smiles

You thought had been evicted from your jawline

Praise the eyes

For seeing and still believing.

For being blinded from faith

But never losing their vision

Praise the visions.

Praise the prophets

Who don't profit off of those visions.

Praise the heart

For housing this living room of emotions

Praise the trophy that is my name

Praise the gift that is my name.

Praise the name that is my name

Which no one can plagiarize or gentrify

Praise the praise.

How the throat sounds like a choir.

The harmony in my tongue lifts

Into a song of adoration.

Praise myself

For being able to praise.

For waking up,

When I had every reason not to.

PERMISSIONS

Grateful acknowledgments are made for permission to include the following poems. All efforts have been made by the editor to contact copyright holders for the material used in this book. The editor regrets any omissions that may have occurred and will correct any such errors in future editions of this book.

"A Love Poem Written for Sterling Brown" by Sonia Sanchez originally appeared in *I've Been a Woman* (1978). Used by permission of the author.

"A New Day Dawns" from *Love Child: Love Child's Hotbed:* Copyright © 2020 by Nikky Finney. Published in 2020 by TriQuarterly Books/Northwestern University Press. Used by permission of the publisher. All rights reserved.

"A Parable of Sorts" by Malika S. Booker, used by permission of the author.

"A Piece of Tail" by Teri Ellen Cross Davis, from *Haint* (Gival Press, 2016). Reprinted by permission of Gival Press.

"a poem about you and me and the new country" by Anis Mojgani, first published in *The Tigers They Let Me* by Anis Mojgani (Write Bloody Press, 2023), used by permission of the author.

"A Twice Named Family" by Traci Dant, used by permission of the author.

"Accents" by Yvette R. Murray, from *I Am a Furious Wish* anthology, used by permission of the author.

"Another Homecoming" by Jarita Davis originally appeared in *Return Flights,* published by Tagus Press in 2016. Used by permission of the author.

"Antebellum" by Gregory Pardlo, originally published in Totem, Copper Canyon Press (2007). Used by permission of the author.

"As Serious as a Heart Attack" by Kalamu ya Salaam, used by permission of the author.

"Aubade to Langston" by Rachel Eliza Griffiths, W. W. Norton & Company (2020). Used by permission of the author.

"Butter" by Elizabeth Alexander from *Crave Radiance: New and Selected Poems 1990–2010,* used by permission of Graywolf Press, Minneapolis, MN, 2010.

"Carl's Barbershop" by Abdul Ali, first published in *Plume,* issue 66, January 2017, used by permission of the author.

"Carolina Prayer" by Justin Phillip Reed, from *Indecency.* Copyright © 2018 by Justin Phillip Reed. Reprinted with the permission of The Permissions Company, LLC, on behalf of Coffee House Press, coffeehousepress.org.

"Characteristics of Life" by Camille T. Dungy, used by permission of the author.

"Condition: If the Garden of Eden Was in Africa" by DéLana R. A. Dameron, from *How God Ends Us* by DéLana R. A. Dameron (University of South Carolina Press, 2009). Used by permission of the author.

"Conjecture on the Stained-Glass Image of White Christ at Ebenezer Baptist Church" by Marcus Wicker, used by permission of the author.

"Contemplating 'Mistress,' Sally in 2017" by Chet'la Sebree, from *Mistress* (2019) by Chet'la Sebree. Used by permission of the author.

"Crows in a Strong Wind" by Cornelius Eady, copyright 1985 Cornelius Eady, used by permission of the author.

"Dear Barbershop," by Chris Slaughter, used by permission of the author.

"Happy" by Kevin Powell, used by permission of the author.

"Harold's Chicken Shack #35" from *Wild Hundreds* by Nate Marshall, University of Pittsburgh Press, 2015, used by permission of the author.

"Healing" by Lolita Stewart-White, used by permission of the author.

"Heaven: For Nikki Giovanni's 80th Birthday" by Renée Watson, used by permission of the author.

"Hello" by Sean Hill, copyright © 2019 by Sean Hill. Originally published in *Poem-a-Day* on December 13, 2019, by the Academy of American Poets. Used by permission of the author.

"Hip Hop Analogies" by Tara Betts first appeared in the April 2015 issue of *Poetry* magazine, just prior to its appearance in *The BreakBeat Poets: New American Poetry in the Age of Hip-Hop* (Haymarket Books, 2015). Used by permission of the author.

"His Presence" by Kwame Dawes, from *Jacko Jacobus* (Peepal Tree Press, 1996) and *New and Selected Poems* (Peepal Tree Press, 2003) © Kwame Dawes, reproduced by permission of Peepal Tree Press.

"Holla" by Evie Shockley, from *Suddenly We* © 2022 by Evie Shockley. Published by Wesleyan University Press. Used by permission.

"How to Get Emotional Distance When Voodoo Is Not an Option" by Pamela L. Taylor first appeared in *Atlas + Alice* on December 3, 2018. Used by permission of the author.

"Inheritance" by Tyree Daye, from the collection *Cardinal* (Copper Canyon Press). Used by permission of the author.

"Inundated" by Hayes Davis, copyright Hayes Davis, used by permission of the author.

"Labor" by Jericho Brown, from *The New Testament* by Jericho Brown, Copper Canyon Press, Port Townsend, WA, 2014, used by permission of the author.

"Love for a Song" by J. Drew Lanham, reprinted from *Sparrow Envy: A Field Guide to Birds and Lesser Beasts* © 2022 by J. Drew Lanham. Permission of Hub City Press. Used by permission of the author.

"Love Poem" by Cameron Awkward-Rich, used by permission of the author.

"'[love letter to self]" by Warsan Shire, used by permission of the author.

"Magnitude and Bond" by Nicole Terez Dutton, used by permission of the author.

"May Perpetual Light Shine" by Patrica Spears Jones was originally published in poets.org. Used by permission of the author.

"Most Beautiful Accident: A Single Parent's Ode" by Samantha Thornhill, previously published in *World Literature Today*. Used by permission of the author.

"Mule" by Sharan Strange from *Ash* (Boston: Beacon Press, 2001). Copyright © 2001 by Sharan Strange. Used with the permission of the author.

"Mussels" by Lucinda Roy, used by permission of the author in care of the Jean V. Naggar Literary Agency, Inc.

"My Father's Geography" from *My Father's Geography* by Michael S. Weaver, published by the University of Pittsburgh Press, 1992.

"My Poems" by Joanna Crowell, used by permission of the author.

"Navel" by Robin Coste Lewis, used by permission of the author.

"Nelsons (On the Road 1957)" by Marilyn Nelson, used by permission of the author.

"Ode to Sudanese-Americans" by Safia Elhillo, used by permission of the author.

"Offertory" by Chris Abani, used by permission of the author.

"oh didn't they tell us we would all have new names when we decided to convert?" by Nikia Chaney, used by permission of the author.

"On Being Called the N-Word in Atlanta, 2016: A Southern Ghazal" by Teri Elam. A slightly different version of this poem was published in the online journals *Limp Wrist* magazine and *Auburn Avenue*. Used by permission of the author.

author's poetry collection, *More God Than Dead,* published by Muddy Ford Press, 2022. Used by permission of the author.

"A Prayer for Workers" by Yusef Komunyakaa, used by permission of the author.

"Quality: Gwendolyn Brooks at 73" by Haki R. Madhubuti, from *Heartlove: Wedding and Love Poems,* Third World Press, Chicago, 1969, used by permission of the author.

"Quare" by L. Lamar Wilson, used by permission of the author.

"Queen Bess" by Kimberly A. Collins, copyright 2018, used by permission of the author.

"Quilting the Black-Eyed Pea" by Nikki Giovanni from *Quilting the Black-Eyed Pea: Poems and Not Quite Poems* by Nikki Giovanni. HarperCollins, 2002. Reprinted by permission of the author.

"R&B Facts" by Nicholas Goodly, used by permission of the author.

"Refractions" by Alan King, used by permission of the author.

"Reunion" by Reginald Harris, from *Autogeography: Poems.* Copyright © 2013 by Reginald Harris. Published 2013 by Northwestern University Press. Used by permission of the author.

"The Ear Is an Organ Made for Love" by E. Ethelbert Miller, used by permission of the author.

"The Gray Mare" by Afaa Michael Weaver, used by permission of the author.

"The I Be Tree" by Truth Thomas, used by permission of the author.

"The Language of Joy" by Jacqueline Allen Trimble, © 2022, from *How to Survive the Apocalypse*. Used by permission of the / University of Georgia Press.

"The Mystery Man in the Black Hat Speaks" by Quincy Troupe from *Errançities*. Copyright © 2012 by Quincy Troupe. Reprinted with the permission of The Permissions Company, LLC, on behalf of Coffee House Press, coffeehousepress.org.

"The Nightflies" by Sheree Renée Thomas, © 2011, appeared in her collection *Shotgun Lullabies: Stories & Poems,* published by Aqueduct Press, Seattle.

"The Origins of the Artist: Natalie Cole" by Toi Derricotte, used by permission of the author.

"The Painter" by Opal Palmer Adisa © 2008 by Opal Palmer Adisa in the collection *I Name Me Name,* Leeds UK: Peepal Tree Press. Used by permission of the author.

"The President Has Never Said the Word *Black*" by Morgan Parker, used by permission of the author.

"The Ragged and the Beautiful" by Safiya Sinclair, reprinted by permission of the author.

"The Talk" by Gayle Danley, used by permission of the author.

"This Is an Incomprehensive List of All the Reasons I Know I Married the Right Person" by Clint Smith, used by permission of the author.

"This Is the Honey" by Mahogany L. Browne, used by permission of the author.

"[this to say i am more terrified of capitalism than any wildlife encounter]" by Jasmine Elizabeth Smith, used by permission of the author.

"To Racism" by Lucinda Roy, used by permission of the author in care of the Jean V. Naggar Literary Agency, Inc.

"tripping" by Van G. Garrett, used by permission of the author.

"Twigi" by Gary Jackson, from *origin story* by Gary Jackson, copyright 2021 Gary Jackson. University of New Mexico Press, 2021.

"Unrest in Baton Rouge" from *Wade in the Water Poems* by Tracy K. Smith, Graywolf Press, Minneapolis, 2018, used by permission of the author.

ABOUT THE POETS

Chris Abani is an acclaimed novelist and poet. His most recent books are *The Secret History of Las Vegas, The Face: Cartography of the Void,* and *Sanctificum.* He has received a Guggenheim Fellowship, the PEN/ Hemingway Award, an Edgar Award, a USA Fellowship, the PEN Beyond Margins Award, a Prince Claus Award, the Hurston/Wright Legacy Award, and a Lannan Literary Fellowship, among many other honors. Born in Nigeria, he is a member of the American Academy of Arts and Sciences and a Board of Trustees Professor of English at Northwestern University. He lives in Chicago.

Elizabeth Acevedo is the *New York Times* bestselling author of *The Poet X,* which won the National Book Award for Young People's Literature, the Michael L. Printz Award, the Pura Belpré Award, the Carnegie Medal, the *Boston Globe*–Horn Book Award, and the Walter Award. She is also the author of *With the Fire on High* and *Clap When You Land,* which was a *Boston Globe*–Horn Book Honor book and a Kirkus finalist. She holds a BA in performing arts from George Washington University and an MFA in creative writing from the University of Maryland. Acevedo has been a fellow of Cave Canem and CantoMundo and a participant in the *Callaloo* Creative Writing Workshops. She is a National Poetry Slam Champion and resides in Washington, DC, with her love.

Opal Palmer Adisa's recent publications include *The Storyteller's Return: Story Poems* (released in March 2022 by Ian Randle Publishers) and *Portia Dreams* (2021), the authorized children's biography of Portia Simpson-Miller, Jamaica's first female prime minister. Adisa is the editor of *100+ Voices for Miss Lou: Poetry, Tributes, Interviews, Essays* (University of the West Indies Press, 2021). She is also the editor in chief of two major journals, *Interviewing the Caribbean* and *Caribbean Conjunctures,* the Caribbean Studies Association journal, containing scholarly essays and book reviews by Caribbean scholars exploring issues that impact the Caribbean. Adisa's essays, stories, poems, and articles have been anthologized in more than five hundred publications. She is professor emerita of the California College of the Arts and has taught at the University of California, Berkeley, Stanford University, and San Francisco State University.

Elizabeth Alexander—poet, educator, memoirist, scholar, and cultural advocate—is president of the Andrew W. Mellon Foundation, the nation's largest funder in arts and culture and humanities in higher education. Dr. Alexander has held distinguished professorships at Smith College, Columbia University, and Yale University, where she taught for fifteen years and chaired the African American Studies department. She is a chancellor of the Academy of American Poets, serves on the Pulitzer Prize Board, and codesigned the Art for Justice Fund. Notably, Alexander composed and delivered the poem "Praise Song for the Day" for the inauguration of President Barack Obama in 2009, and she is also the author or coauthor of fourteen books. Her book of poems *American Sublime* was a finalist for the Pulitzer Prize for Poetry in 2006, and her memoir, *The Light of the World,* was a finalist for the Pulitzer Prize for Biography in 2015.

Abdul Ali is the author of *Trouble Sleeping* (2015), winner of the New Issues Poetry Prize, selected by poet Fanny Howe. His poetry, essays, and interviews have appeared in *Gargoyle*, *Gathering of Tribes*, the *Washington Post Magazine*, *New Contrast* (South Africa), and *Poet Lore*, on National Public Radio, on the websites of the Academy of American Poets and the Poetry Foundation, and in the anthology *Full Moon on K Street: Poems About Washington DC* (2009) and other publications. He has taught writing at Towson University and Goucher College and currently teaches in the graduate writing program at Johns Hopkins University.

A$iahMae is a writer, producer, performing poet, community curator, and organizer living in Charleston, South Carolina. They were named Charleston's second poet laureate in 2022 and says, "I've been writing since the day I learned how to spell my name. It was like, oh! Words! I can do something with this. I was really shy as a kid, so journaling and writing poetry helped me to say the things I wanted to say." Radical healing and love, joy as resistance, community, family, queerness, blackness, and sustainability are all themes that A$iahMae incorporates into their poetry. As poet laureate, they are working to put out more collaborative projects and to promote poetry in more spaces. Most important, they continue to push for artists to be able to live and thrive in their communities.

Jabari Asim is the recipient of a Guggenheim Fellowship in Creative Arts and the author of seven books for adults, including *We Can't Breathe: On Black Lives, White Lies, and the Art of Survival* and ten books for children. His poems are included in several anthologies, including *Furious Flower: African American Poetry from the Black Arts Movement to the Present*; *Beyond the Frontier: African American Poetry for the 21st Century*; and

Role Call: A Generational Anthology of Social & Political Black Literature and Art. After more than a decade at the *St. Louis Post-Dispatch* and the *Washington Post*, he now directs the MFA program at Emerson College.

Derrick Austin was born in Homestead, Florida. He received a BA from the University of Tampa and, in 2014, an MFA from the University of Michigan. He is the author of *Tenderness* (BOA Editions, 2021), winner of the 2021 Isabella Gardner Award, and *Trouble the Water* (BOA Editions, 2016), selected by Mary Szybist for the 2015 A. Poulin Jr. Poetry Prize. A Cave Canem fellow, he is also the recipient of fellowships from the Wisconsin Institute for Creative Writing and Stanford University. He currently lives in Oakland, California.

Cameron Awkward-Rich is the author of two collections of poetry—*Sympathetic Little Monster* and *Dispatch*—as well as *The Terrible We: Thinking with Trans Maladjustment*. His work has been supported by fellowships from Cave Canem, the Lannan Foundation, and the American Council of Learned Societies. He currently teaches in the Women, Gender, Sexuality Studies department at the University of Massachusetts Amherst.

Dr. Joshua Bennett is the author of *The Sobbing School*, which was a National Poetry Series selection and a finalist for an NAACP Image Award. He is also the author of *Being Property Once Myself*, *Owed*, and *Spoken Word: A Cultural History*. He has received fellowships and awards from the Guggenheim Foundation, the Whiting Foundation, the National Endowment for the Arts, and the Society of Fellows at Harvard University. He is a professor of literature and distinguished chair of the humanities at MIT.

Reginald Dwayne Betts, poet and lawyer, is the author of three collections of poetry: *Felon, Bastards of the Reagan Era,* and *Shahid Reads His Own Palm.* A 2021 MacArthur fellow, he is the executive director of Freedom Reads, a not-for-profit organization that is radically transforming access to literature in prisons through the installation of "freedom libraries" in prisons across the country.

Tara Betts is the author of *Refuse to Disappear, Break the Habit,* and *Arc & Hue.* She teaches at DePaul University and lives in Chicago. Her poems have appeared in many anthologies and magazines.

Remica Bingham-Risher is the author of three poetry collections, including *Starlight & Error* and *What We Ask of Flesh,* as well as *Soul Culture: Black Poets, Books, and Questions That Grew Me Up,* a collection of essays. Bingham-Risher is the director of quality enhancement plan initiatives at Old Dominion University, which means she helps faculty integrate writing into the classroom. Bingham-Risher lives in Norfolk, Virginia.

Toni Blackman is the author of the poetry collection *Inner-course.* An international champion of hip-hop culture, known for the irresistible, contagious energy of her performances and alluring female presence, she was named by the US Department of State as the first ever hip-hop artist to work as an American Cultural Specialist. She has served in Senegal, Ghana, Botswana, and Swaziland, where her residencies included performance, workshops, and lectures on hip-hop music and culture. She has shared the stage with artists including Erykah Badu, Mos Def, The Roots, Wu Tang Clan, Guru, Bahamadia, Boot Camp Clik, Meshell Ndegeocello, Sarah McLachlan, Sheryl Crow, Jill Sobule, and Rickie Lee Jones.

Nadir Lasana Bomani is a Baba, husband, poet, educator, and photographer, born and raised in the city that makes roux. His work appears in *100 Best African American Poems, Beyond the Frontier, A Deeper Shade of Sex, Fertile Ground, I Am New Orleans,* and *Thicker Than Water: A Marriage Between Poetry and Prose,* cowritten with Mawiyah Kai EL-Jamah Bomani.

Malika S. Booker is an international writer whose work is steeped in anthropological research methodology and rooted in storytelling. Her writing spans poetry, theater, monologue, installation, and education. Clients and organizations she has worked with include Arts Council England, the BBC, British Council, Wellcome Trust, National Theatre, Royal Shakespeare Company, Arvon, and Hampton Court Palace.

Antoinette Brim-Bell's most recent book is *These Women You Gave Me.* She is a professor of English at Capital Community College in Hartford, Connecticut. In 2022, Brim-Bell was appointed state poet laureate of Connecticut.

LeRonn P. Brooks is an artist, poet, and the curator of the African American Art History Initiative at the Getty Research Institute in Los Angeles.

Jericho Brown is the author of *The Tradition,* for which he won the Pulitzer Prize. He is the recipient of fellowships from the Guggenheim Foundation, the Radcliffe Institute for Advanced Study at Harvard, and the National Endowment for the Arts, and he is a winner of the Whiting Award. Brown's first book, *Please,* won the American Book Award; his second book, *The New Testament* (Copper Canyon, 2014), won the Anisfield-Wolf Book Award; and his third collection, *The Tradition,* won the Paterson Poetry Prize and was a finalist for the National Book Award and the National Book Critics Circle Award. His poems have appeared in the *Bennington Review, Buzzfeed, Fence, Jubilat,* the *New Republic,* the *New York Times, The New Yorker,* the *Paris Review, Time,* and several volumes of *The Best American Poetry.* He is the director of the creative writing program and a professor at Emory University.

Mahogany L. Browne is the executive director of JustMedia, a media literacy initiative designed to support the groundwork of criminal justice leaders and community members. This position is informed by her career as a writer, organizer, and educator. She is the author of the recent works *Chlorine Sky, Woke: A Young Poet's Call to Justice, Woke Baby,* and *Black Girl Magic.*

CM Burroughs is an associate professor of poetry at Columbia College Chicago. She is the author of two collections, *The Vital System* and *Master Suffering,* which was long-listed for the National Book Award and a finalist for both the Los Angeles Times Book Prize and Lambda Literary Award.

Dr. Taylor Byas, PhD, is a Black Chicago native currently living in Cincinnati, where she is an assistant features editor for *The Rumpus,* an acquisitions poetry editor for *Variant Literature,* and a member of the *Beloit Poetry Journal* editorial board. She is the first-place winner of the 2020 Poetry Super Highway, the 2020 Frontier Poetry Award for New Poets, and the 2021 Adrienne Rich Award for Poetry, and she was a finalist for the 2020 Frontier OPEN. She is the author of the collection *I Done Clicked My Heels Three Times.* She is also a coeditor of *Poemhood: Our Black Revival,* a YA anthology.

Nikia Chaney is a multi-genre author and artist. She has published two poetry books, *to stir &* and *us mouth,* a memoir, *Ladybug,* and a short volume of science fiction, *Three Walking.* She teaches in Santa Cruz.

Cortney Lamar Charleston is the author of *Telepathologies* and *Doppelgangbanger.* He has received fellowships from Cave Canem, the New Jersey State Council on the Arts, and the Poetry Foundation.

Pearl Cleage is an Atlanta-based writer whose work has won commercial acceptance and critical praise in several genres. An award-winning playwright whose *Flyin' West* was the most produced new play in the country in 1994, Cleage is also a bestselling author whose first novel, *What Looks Like Crazy on an Ordinary Day,* was an Oprah's Book Club pick. Her subsequent novels, *I Wish I Had a Red Dress* and *Some Things I Never Thought I'd Do,* have been consistent bestsellers and perennial book club favorites. Her poem *We Speak Your Names,* a poetic celebration commissioned by Oprah Winfrey and coauthored with her husband, writer Zaron W. Burnett, Jr., was an *NAACP Image Award* nominee in 2007.

Ama Codjoe is the author of *Bluest Nude,* winner of the Lenore Marshall Poetry Prize and finalist for the NAACP Image Award for Outstanding Poetry and the Paterson Poetry Prize, and *Blood of the Air,* winner of the Drinking Gourd Chapbook Poetry Prize. Among numerous honors, she is the winner of a 2023 Whiting Award.

Gerald L. Coleman is a philosopher, theologian, poet, and science fiction and fantasy author. He is a Scholastic Art and Writing Award juror, a cofounder of the Affrilachian Poets, a member of the Science Fiction and

Fantasy Writers Association, a Rhysling Award nominee, and a fellow at the Black Earth Institute. His newest releases include a collection of short stories entitled *From Earth and Sky* and a collection of poems and micro-essays entitled *On the Black Hand Side.*

Kimberly A. Collins is a Callaloo fellow and Pushcart finalist who teaches English at Howard University. She is the author of two books of poetry, *Bessie's Resurrection* and *Slightly Off Center,* as well as a collection of essays, *Choose You! Wednesday Wisdom to Wake Your Soul.* She is a native of Philadelphia who currently resides in Washington, DC.

Curtis L. Crisler was born and raised in Gary, Indiana. An award-winning poet and author, he has written six poetry books, two YA books, and five poetry chapbooks. He has been an editor and contributing poetry editor. He is also the creator of the Indiana Chitlin Circuit and the poetry form called the sonastic, and he is a professor of English at Purdue University Fort Wayne.

Joanna Crowell is the founder of Ascension Theatre and the Women Writing from Experience workshop series, where she facilitated creative writing workshops for women and teens and created a platform for them to perform and share their stories. She was a professional actress for more than twenty years, having been a member of numerous theater companies. She earned a BA in women's studies and feminist research as well as social justice and peace studies from the University of Western Ontario. She is the author of a book of poems called *I Ate a Rainbow for Breakfast* and the play *AWOL: A Soldier's Journey,* produced by PURE Theatre in 2011.

DéLana R. A. Dameron is the author of the novel *Redwood Court.* Her debut poetry collection, *How God Ends Us,* was selected by Elizabeth Alexander for the 2008 South Carolina Poetry Book Prize, and her second collection, *Weary Kingdom,* was selected by Nikky Finney for the Palmetto Poetry Series. Dameron is the founder of Saloma Acres, a 22.5-acre equestrian and cultural play space she established in her hometown of Columbia, South Carolina, in 2021.

Gayle Danley is a poet who, after winning the International Poetry Slam in Heidelberg, Germany, entered America's classrooms, teaching children the power of words as an aid in healing trauma and creating a life of hope and options. Her work as a teaching artist has been profiled on *60 Minutes* and in the *Baltimore Sun,* the *Washington Post,* and the *New York Times.* Danley served as the Maryland Library Association Poet of the Year and is a former national Young Audiences Artist of the Year.

Traci Dant is the author of *Some Kind of Love: A Family Reunion in Poems.* Her novel in progress, *Polio Summer,* has won support from the Sustainable Arts Foundation and the Society of Children's Book Writers and Illustrators. Dant has also received fellowships from the MacDowell Colony and the Cave Canem Foundation.

Kyle G. Dargan is the author of five collections of poetry, most recently, *Anagnorisis, Honest Engine,* and *Logorrhea Dementia.* His debut, *The Listening* (University of Georgia Press, 2004), won the 2003 Cave Canem Prize, and his second, *Bouquet of Hungers* (University of Georgia Press, 2007), was awarded the 2008 Hurston/Wright Legacy Award in poetry. Dargan's poems and nonfiction have appeared in publications such as

Callaloo, the *Denver Quarterly, Jubilat,* the *Star-Ledger, Ploughshares, The Root.com,* and *Shenandoah.* While a Yusef Komunyakaa fellow at Indiana University, he served as poetry editor for *Indiana Review.* He is the founding editor of the *Post No Ills* magazine and was most recently the managing editor of *Callaloo.*

Dr. Michael Datcher received his BS from the University of California, Berkeley, and his PhD in English literature from the University of California, Riverside. He is the author of the *New York Times* bestseller *Raising Fences* and the critically acclaimed Ferguson-area historical novel *Americus.* His book *Animating Black and Brown Liberation: A Theory of American Literatures* was nominated for the Pulitzer Prize. Datcher has made numerous media appearances, including on *Oprah,* the *Today* show, and *Dateline.* Dr. Datcher is a clinical assistant professor of writing at New York University's School of Liberal Studies.

Hayes Davis holds an MFA from the University of Maryland. He is a member of Cave Canem's first cohort of fellows, a former Bread Loaf working scholar, and a former Geraldine Miles Poet-Scholar at the Squaw Valley Community of Writers. His first volume of poems, *Let Our Eyes Linger,* was published by Poetry Mutual Press in April 2016. His work has appeared in *New England Review, Poet Lore, Gargoyle, Delaware Poetry Review, Kinfolks,* and several anthologies. He teaches English at Sidwell Friends School in Washington, DC, and lives in Silver Spring with his wife, the poet Teri Ellen Cross Davis, and their children.

Jarita Davis is a poet and fiction writer with a BA from Brown University and an MA and a PhD from the University of Louisiana, Lafayette. Her work has appeared in the *Southwestern Review, Cave Canem Anthologies, Crab Orchard Review, Plainsongs, Verdad Magazine,* and the *Cape Cod Poetry Review.* She lives and writes in West Falmouth, Massachusetts.

Teri Ellen Cross Davis is the author of *a more perfect Union* (2019), winner of the Journal/Charles B. Wheeler Poetry Prize), and *Haint* (2017), winner of the Ohioana Book Award for Poetry. She is the 2020 Poetry Society of America's Robert H. Winner Memorial Award winner. She curates the O. B. Hardison Poetry Series and is the poetry programs manager for the Folger Shakespeare Library in Washington, DC.

Kwame Dawes is the author of twenty books of poetry, including *City of Bones: A Testament,* and numerous other works of fiction, criticism, and essays. In 2016 his book *Speak from Here to There,* a collection of verse cowritten with Australian poet John Kinsella, was published. He is the Glenna Luschei editor in chief of *Prairie Schooner* and teaches at the University of Nebraska and the Pacific University MFA program. He is also the director of the African Poetry Book Fund and the artistic director of the Calabash International Literary Festival.

Tyree Daye was raised in Youngsville, North Carolina. He is the author of the poetry collections *a little bump in the earth, Cardinal,* and *River Hymns,* winner of the APR/Honickman First Book Prize.

Marlanda Dekine is a poet, a voice, and a presence. She is the author of *Thresh & Hold* and *i am from a punch & a kiss.* Her work has been anthologized in *What Things Cost: An Anthology for the People* and *Ecological Solidarities: Mobilizing Faith and Justice in an Entangled World.* She is a

South Carolina Spoken Word Poetry fellow, a *Tin House* scholar, and a Palm Beach Poetry Langston Hughes fellow. Her poems have been set to music by composers and published by the Poetry Foundation and in *American Life in Poetry*, the *Oxford American*, and other publications.

Toi Derricotte's sixth collection of poetry, *I: New and Selected Poems*, was short-listed for the 2019 National Book Award. She was awarded the Frost Medal from the Poetry Society of America in 2020 and the Wallace Stevens Award from the Academy of American Poets in 2021. With Cornelius Eady, she cofounded Cave Canem, a home for the many voices of African American poetry, in 1996.

Joel Dias-Porter, aka DJ Renegade, is the author of *Ideas of Improvisation* and the recipient of a Furious Flower Poetry Prize. He lives in Atlantic City.

Mitchell L. H. Douglas is the author of *dying in the scarecrow's arms*, *\blak\ \al-fə bet*, winner of the Persea Books Lexi Rudnitsky Editor's Choice Award, and *Cooling Board: A Long-Playing Poem*, an NAACP Image Award and Hurston/Wright Legacy Award nominee. His poetry has appeared in *Callaloo*, *The Ringing Ear: Black Poets Lean South*, *The BreakBeat Poets: New American Poetry in the Age of Hip-Hop*, *Crab Orchard Review*, and *Ninth Letter*, among other publications. He is a cofounder of the Affrilachian Poets, a Cave Canem graduate, and an associate professor of English at Indiana University–Purdue University Indianapolis.

Rita Dove is a Pulitzer Prize–winning poet and former US poet laureate whose latest collection is *Playlist for the Apocalypse*. She is the Henry Hoyns Professor of Creative Writing in the English department at the University of Virginia.

Camille T. Dungy is the author of four collections of poetry. Her interest in the intersections between literature, environmental action, history, and culture led her to edit *Black Nature: Four Centuries of African American Nature Poetry* (University of Georgia Press, 2009), the first anthology to bring African American environmental poetry to national attention. She also coedited the *From the Fishouse* poetry anthology and has served in several other editorial positions. Currently she is the poetry editor for *Orion* magazine. Dungy's work has appeared in more than forty anthologies plus dozens of print and online venues in the US and abroad. She is the host of *Immaterial,* a podcast from the Metropolitan Museum of Art and Magnificent Noise. Dungy's honors include the 2021 Academy of American Poets Fellowship, a 2019 Guggenheim Fellowship, an American Book Award, two NAACP Image Award nominations, and fellowships from the National Endowment for the Arts in both prose and poetry. She is a University Distinguished Professor at Colorado State University.

Nicole Terez Dutton's work has appeared in *Callaloo, Ploughshares, 32 Poems, Indiana Review,* and *Salt Hill Journal.* Dutton earned an MFA from Brown University and has received fellowships from The Frost Place, the Fine Arts Work Center, Bread Loaf Writers' Conference, and the Virginia Center for the Creative Arts. Her collection of poems, *If One of Us Should Fall,* won the 2011 Cave Canem Poetry Prize. She teaches in the Solstice Low-Residency MFA program and is the editor of the *Kenyon Review.*

Cornelius Eady, poet, playwright, and songwriter, was born in Rochester, New York. His second book, *Victims of the Latest Dance Craze,* won the 1985 Lamont Prize from the Academy of American Poets. His libretto for

Deidre Murray's opera *Running Man* was short-listed for the 1992 Pulitzer Prize. A cofounder of the Cave Canem workshop, he currently holds the Hodges Chair of Excellence at the University of Tennessee, Knoxville.

Mary Moore Easter is a Cave Canem fellow and professor of dance emerita at Carleton College. Her chapbook is *Walking from Origins.*

teri elam's poetry can be found in *Let Me Say This, Prairie Schooner,* and *december* magazine. As a screenwriter, she has been both a SAGindie Finalist and ScreenCraft semifinalist. A Tuskegee University alumna, she has an EdM from the University of Georgia and a Stonecoast MFA at the University of Southern Maine.

Safia Elhillo is an award-winning poet and author. Her debut YA novel in verse, *Home Is Not a Country,* was long-listed for the National Book Award and received a Coretta Scott King Book Award Author Honor and an Arab American Book Award. Sudanese by way of Washington, DC, Elhillo is a Pushcart Prize nominee and cowinner of the 2015 Brunel International African Poetry Prize, and she is listed in *Forbes Africa*'s 2018 "30 Under 30." She lives in Los Angeles.

Inua Ellams is an award-winning poet, playwright, and curator. Identity, displacement, and destiny are recurring themes in his work, in which he mixes the old with the new, the traditional with the contemporary. Born in Nigeria, he is the author of the poetry books *Candy Coated Unicorn and Converse All Stars, The Wire-Headed Heathen, The Half God of Rainfall,* and *The Actual.* His plays include *Black T-shirt Collection, The 14th Tale, Barber Shop Chronicles,* and *Three Sisters.*

Chanda Feldman is the author of *Approaching the Fields*. She is an assistant professor of creative writing at Oberlin College.

Nikky Finney is the author of *On Wings Made of Gauze, Rice, The World Is Round,* and *Head Off & Split,* which won the National Book Award for Poetry in 2011. Her collection of poems *Love Child's Hotbed of Occasional Poetry* was released in 2020. Finney is Carolina Distinguished Professor at the University of South Carolina in Columbia, where she is also director of the Ernest A. Finney, Jr. Cultural Arts Center.

Aricka Foreman is an American poet and interdisciplinary writer from Detroit. Author of the chapbooks *Dream with a Glass Chamber* and *Salt Body Shimmer,* she has earned fellowships from Cave Canem, *Callaloo,* and the Millay Colony for the Arts. She serves on the board of directors for *The Offing* and spends her time in Chicago, engaging poetry with photography and video.

Ruth Forman is the author of the bestselling children's books *Curls, Glow, Bloom, Ours, One,* and *Like So,* as well as the award-winning poetry collections *We Are the Young Magicians* and *Renaissance.*

Jonterri Gadson is a former creative writing professor who chose TV over tenure. She is currently a writer on Viacom's *Everybody Still Hates Chris* and has also written for Netflix's *The Upshaws,* HBO's *A Black Lady Sketch Show,* NBC's *Making It,* with Amy Poehler and Nick Offerman, *The Kelly Clarkson Show,* and Adult Swim's half-hour comedy *Bird Girl.* Additionally, she was a comedy consulting producer on *12 Dates of Christmas* (HBO Max), writing comedic host copy for Natasha Rothwell, and a writer for NBC's *Ultimate Slip 'N Slide,* writing comedic host copy for Bobby Moynihan and Ron Funches. She won Kevin Hart's LOL Film Fellowship for a short she wrote and directed that premiered at the American Black Film Festival. She has published three poetry books, including the collection *Blues Triumphant.*

Van G. Garrett is the winner of the 2020 Poetry Question Chapbook Contest for his book *Scrap.* He is also the winner of the 2017 Best Book of African American Poetry for his book *49: Wings and Prayers,* as announced by the Texas Association of Authors. Garrett is also the author of thirteen books and the poetry collections *Songs in Blue Negritude; Lennox in Twelve; Hog;* and *Zuri: Love Songs.* His debut picture book, *Kicks,* an ode to the flyest shoes and those who wear them, was published in 2022 (Versify/HarperCollins). His second picture book, *Juneteenth,* was also published by Versify/HarperCollins, in the summer of 2023. Garrett's updates and appearances can be found at vanggarrettpoet.com.

Ross Gay is the author of four books of poetry: *Against Which, Bringing the Shovel Down, Be Holding,* winner of the PEN/Jean Stein Book Award, and *Catalog of Unabashed Gratitude,* winner of the 2015 National Book Critics Circle Award and the 2016 Kingsley Tufts Poetry Award. In addition to his poetry, Gay has released three collections of essays — *The Book of Delights* (2019), which was a *New York Times* bestseller; *Inciting Joy* (2022); and *The Book of (More) Delights* (2023).

Angelo Geter is an award-winning poet and teaching artist currently serving as the poet laureate of Rock Hill, South Carolina. Geter is a 2020 Academy of American Poets Laureate Fellow and a National Poetry Slam champion. His debut collection, *More God Than Dead,* was published in 2022.

Brian Gilmore is a poet, writer, and columnist with the Progressive Media Project. He is the author of three collections of poetry: *Elvis Presley is alive and well and living in Harlem, Jungle Nights and Soda Fountain Rags: Poem for Duke Ellington,* and *We Didn't Know Any Gangsters.* His poems and writings are widely published and have appeared in *The Progressive,* the *Washington Post,* the *Baltimore Sun, Sugar House Review,* and *Jubilat.* Currently he teaches law at the Michigan State University College of Law. He divides his time between Michigan and his beloved birthplace, Washington, DC.

Nikki Giovanni, an activist, mother, professor, and world-renowned poet, is a seven-time NAACP Image Award winner, the first recipient of the Rosa Parks Woman of Courage Award, and a winner of the Langston Hughes Medal for Outstanding Poetry. The recipient of many other honors as well, she is the author of twenty-eight books of poetry for children and adults, including *Ego-Tripping and Other Poems for Young People, I Am Loved, Make Me Rain, Quilting the Black-Eyed Pea,* and *A Good Cry.* A Grammy nominee for *The Nikki Giovanni Poetry Collection,* she is the former University Distinguished Professor of English at Virginia Tech.

Nicholas Goodly is the author of *Black Swim.* They are a team member of the performing arts platform *Fly on a Wall* and poetry editor for the *Southeast Review.* Nicholas was a finalist for the 2020 Jake Adam York Prize, runner-up for the 2019 Cave Canem Poetry Prize, and recipient of the 2017 Poetry Society of America Chapbook Fellowship, among other awards. Their work has appeared in *The New Yorker, Boston Review, BOMB,* the *Poetry Project, Lambda Literary,* and *Narrative Magazine.*

Amanda Gorman is the youngest presidential inaugural poet in US history. She is a committed advocate for the environment, racial equality, and gender justice. Amanda's activism and poetry have been featured on the *Today* show, *PBS Kids*, and *CBS This Morning* and in the *New York Times*, *Vogue*, *Essence*, and *O, The Oprah Magazine*. In 2017, Urban Word named her the first-ever National Youth Poet Laureate of the United States. She graduated cum laude from Harvard University and lives in her hometown of Los Angeles. The special edition of her inaugural poem, "The Hill We Climb," was published in March 2021 and debuted at #1 on the *New York Times*, *USA Today*, and *Wall Street Journal* bestseller lists.

Rachel Eliza Griffiths is a poet, novelist, and visual artist. Griffiths is the author of the novel *Promise* and a recipient of the Hurston/Wright Legacy Award for her poetry collection *Seeing the Body*. She lives in New York City.

Nikki Grimes was the recipient of the 2022 Virginia Hamilton Lifetime Achievement Award, the 2020 ALAN Award for outstanding contributions to young adult literature, the 2017 Children's Literature Legacy Award, the 2016 Virginia Hamilton Literary Award, and the 2006 NCTE Award for Excellence in Poetry for Children. Her distinguished works include the much-honored *Garvey's Choice*, ALA Notable book *Southwest Sunrise*, Coretta Scott King Award winner *Bronx Masquerade*, five Coretta Scott King Author Honor books, Printz and Siebert Honor winner *Ordinary Hazards*, and *Boston Globe*–Horn Book Award winner *One Last Word* and its companion *Legacy: Women Poets of the Harlem Renaissance*. Creator of the popular children's books *Meet Danitra Brown*, *Make Way for Dyamonde Daniel*, *Bedtime for Sweet Creatures*, and *Off to See the Sea*, Grimes lives in Corona, California.

Reginald Harris won the 2012 Cave Canem/Northwestern University Press Poetry Prize for Autogeography. He has been the recipient of

Individual Artist Awards for poetry and fiction from the Maryland State Arts Council and a finalist for a Lambda Literary Award for *10 Tongues: Poems* (2002), and his work has appeared in numerous journals, anthologies, and online. He lives in Brooklyn with his partner.

Terrance Hayes's publications include *American Sonnets for My Past and Future Assassin* and *To Float in the Space Between: Drawings and Essays in Conversation with Etheridge Knight,* which was the winner of the Poetry Foundation's 2019 Pegasus Award for Poetry Criticism and a finalist for the 2018 National Book Critics Circle Award in Criticism. *American Sonnets for My Past and Future Assassin* won the 2019 Hurston/Wright Legacy Award for Poetry and was a finalist for the 2018 National Book Critics Circle Award in Poetry, the 2018 National Book Award in Poetry, the 2018 T. S. Eliot Prize for Poetry, and the 2018 Kingsley Tufts Poetry Award. His most recent books are a collection of poems, *So to Speak,* and a collection of essays, *Watch Your Language.* Hayes is a Silver Professor of English at New York University.

Niki Herd is the author of the poetry collection *The Language of Shedding Skin* and the chapbook *don't you weep* and coeditor with Meg Day of *Laura Hershey: On the Life & Work of an American Master.* Herd's poetry, essays, and criticism have appeared in *Gulf Coast,* the *Oxford Research Encyclopedia of Literature,* the *New England Review, Copper Nickel,* the Academy of American Poets' *Poem-a-Day* series, *Lit Hub, The Rumpus, Obsidian,* and *Tupelo Quarterly,* among other journals and anthologies. Her work has been supported by MacDowell, Ucross, Bread Loaf, the Newberry Library, and Cave Canem. Her second full-length poetry collection is *The Stuff of Hollywood.*

Sean Hill is the author of *Dangerous Goods* and *Blood Ties & Brown Liquor*. He has received numerous awards, including fellowships from Cave Canem, the Region 2 Arts Council, the Bush Foundation, the Minnesota State Arts Board, the Jerome Foundation, the MacDowell Colony, the University of Wisconsin, and Stanford University. His poems have appeared in *Callaloo, Harvard Review,* the *Oxford American, Poetry, Tin House,* and numerous other journals and in several anthologies, including *Black Nature* and *Villanelles.* Hill is an editor at Broadsided Press, a monthly broadside publisher. He is currently a visiting professor in the creative writing program at the University of Alaska, Fairbanks.

Gary Jackson is the author of *Missing You, Metropolis,* which was selected by Yusef Komunyakaa as winner of the 2009 Cave Canem Poetry Prize. He teaches in the MFA program at the College of Charleston in South Carolina.

Reuben Jackson is an archivist with the University of the District of Columbia's Felix E. Grant Jazz Archives. He is also the author of two volumes of poetry: *Fingering the Keys* and *Scattered Clouds.* He lives in Washington, DC.

Tyehimba Jess was born in Detroit and earned a BA from the University of Chicago and an MFA from New York University. He is the author of *Olio,* winner of the 2017 Pulitzer Prize for Poetry, and *leadbelly,* winner of the 2004 National Poetry Series. Jess has received a National Endowment for the Arts Fellowship, a Provincetown Fine Arts Work Center Fellowship, and a Whiting Award. He is the poetry and fiction editor of *African American Review* and an associate professor of English at the College of Staten Island.

Jacqueline Johnson is a multidisciplinary artist, creating in poetry, fiction writing, and fiber arts. She is the author of *A Woman's Season* (Main Street Rag) and *A Gathering of Mother Tongues* (White Pine Press). Her works in progress include *The Privilege of Memory*, a novel, and *How to Stop a Hurricane*, a collection of short stories.

Patricia Spears Jones is a poet, playwright, anthologist, educator, and cultural activist. She was the winner of the 2017 Jackson Poetry Prize from Poets & Writers and is the author of *A Lucent Fire: New and Selected Poems*. Her work is anthologized in *African American Poetry: 250 Years of Struggle and Song*, *Of Poetry and Protest: From Emmett Till to Trayvon Martin*, and *BAX 2016: Best American Experimental Writing*. Her poems have been published in *The New Yorker*, the *Brooklyn Rail*, the *Ocean State Review*, *Ms.*, and *Cutthroat*. She edited *THINK: Poems for Aretha Franklin's Inauguration Day Hat* and *Ordinary Women: An Anthology of New York City Women*. Mabou Mines commissioned and produced her plays *Mother* and *Song for New York: What Women Do While Men Sit Knitting*. She has taught graduate and undergraduate creative writing at Hollins University, Adelphi University, Hunter College, and Barnard College. She leads poetry workshops for the 92nd Street Y, The Workroom, Hugo House, Community of Writers, Truro Center for the Arts at Castle Hill, Gemini Ink, and Brooklyn Poets. She organizes the American Poets Congress and is a senior fellow emerita of the Black Earth Institute.

Saeed Jones is the author of the memoir *How We Fight for Our Lives*, winner of the 2019 Kirkus Prize for Nonfiction, and the poetry collection *Prelude to Bruise*, winner of the 2015 PEN/Joyce Osterweil Award for Poetry. His poetry and essays have appeared in *The New Yorker*, the

New York Times, Oxford American, and *GQ,* among other publications. His latest poetry collection is *Alive at the End of the World* (2022).

A. Van Jordan is the author of five collections: *Rise,* which won the PEN Oakland/Josephine Miles Literary Award; *M-A-C-N-O-L-I-A,* which was listed as one the Best Books of 2005 by the *London Times; Quantum Lyrics; The Cineaste;* and *When I Waked, I Cried to Dream Again.* Jordan has been awarded a Whiting Award, an Anisfield-Wolf Book Award, and a Pushcart Prize. He is also the recipient of a Guggenheim Fellowship and a United States Artists Fellowship. He is the Henry Rutgers Presidential Professor at Rutgers University–Newark.

Allison Joseph received a BA from Kenyon College and an MFA from Indiana University Bloomington. She is the author of several poetry collections, including *Confessions of a Barefaced Woman, Worldly Pleasures,* and *What Keeps Us Here,* winner of the John C. Zacharis First Book Award. Joseph has received fellowships and awards from the Illinois Arts Council. She teaches at and directs the MFA in creative writing program at Southern Illinois University Carbondale, where she also serves as the editor in chief and poetry editor of *Crab Orchard Review.* She lives in Carbondale, Illinois.

Alan King is a husband, father, and artist who lives with his family in Bowie, Maryland. He is an author, award-winning documentary filmmaker, and poet. King is a visiting author for the PEN/Faulkner Writers in Schools program, helping to inspire the next generation of readers and writers. His visits through PEN/Faulkner, as one teacher put it, help young people "see literature as it happens, rather than as it happened in history." King's honors include fellowships from Cave Canem and the

Voices of Our Nations Arts Foundation, three Pushcart Prize nominations, and three nominations for *The Best of the Net* anthology.

Yusef Komunyakaa was born in Bogalusa, Louisiana. The son of a carpenter, he was first alerted to the power of language through his grandparents, who were church people; the sound of the Old Testament informed the cadences of their speech, Komunyakaa has stated. "It was my first introduction to poetry." He has taught at numerous institutions, including the University of New Orleans, Indiana University, and Princeton University. He is a senior faculty member in the New York University creative writing program.

Kurtis Lamkin says poetry saved him at age eight. "Being a poet was in my bones," he says. A father at sixteen, married at nineteen, he worked several jobs to take care of his family. When that wasn't enough to make ends meet, he reluctantly resorted to burglary, all the while knowing that was not his path. Reading a book by Langston Hughes changed the direction of his life, making him realize that poetry was what he was destined to do. He is now an accomplished poet and musician, using his voice to uplift and educate.

J. Drew Lanham is an alumni distinguished professor of wildlife ecology, master teacher, and certified wildlife biologist at Clemson University. He is the poet laureate of Edgefield County, South Carolina, where he grew up. He is the author of *The Home Place: Memoirs of a Colored Man's Love Affair with Nature* and a collection of poetry and meditations, *Sparrow Envy: Field Guide to Birds and Lesser Beasts*.

Rickey Laurentiis grew up in New Orleans and earned an MFA from Washington University in St. Louis. They are the author of *Boy with Thorn* (University of Pittsburgh Press), selected by Terrance Hayes for the 2014 Cave Canem Poetry Prize. *Boy with Thorn* also won the Levis Reading Prize and was a finalist for the Kate Tufts Discovery Award, the Thom Gunn Award, and the Lambda Literary Award. A 2012 Ruth Lilly Poetry fellow, they have also received awards from the Whiting Foundation, the Lannan Foundation, the Civitella Ranieri Foundation, and the National Endowment for the Arts. They are the inaugural fellow in creative writing at the University of Pittsburgh's Center for African American Poetry and Poetics.

Len Lawson is the author of *Negro Asylum for the Lunatic Insane* and *Chime.* He is also the coeditor of *The Future of Black: Afrofuturism, Black Comics, and Superhero Poetry.*

Robin Coste Lewis is the author of *Voyage of the Sable Venus,* winner of the National Book Award for Poetry. Her work has appeared in various journals and anthologies, including the *Massachusetts Review, Callaloo,* the *Harvard Gay & Lesbian Review, Transition,* and *VIDA.* Lewis earned her MFA from NYU's creative writing program, where she was a Goldwater fellow in poetry. She also earned an MTS degree in Sanskrit and comparative religious literature from Harvard Divinity School. She is a Cave Canem fellow and was awarded a Provost's Fellowship in the creative writing and literature PhD program at the University of Southern California. Lewis has taught at Wheaton College, Hunter College, and Hampshire College and at New York University's Low-Residency MFA Writers Workshop in Paris. She was born in Compton, California, to a family from New Orleans.

Haki Madhubuti (born Don Lee) embodies the true spirit of a renaissance man as he moves seamlessly through the worlds of literature, business, and education. Detroit-born and raised in Chicago, Madhubuti, a poet, essayist, and entrepreneur, is the author of more than twenty books of poetry, essays, and criticism. Along with two partners he founded the Third World Press in the basement of his Chicago apartment with $400 and a mimeograph machine. A leading figure in the Black Arts Movement, he has become one of the most prominent African American authors of his time without having ever relied on a larger, more established publishing company. Madhubuti and his wife, Safisha, are the founders of the Institute of Positive Education/New Concept School, and he is the recipient of fellowships from both the National Endowment for the Arts and the National Endowment for the Humanities.

Clarence Major is the author of eleven novels, sixteen collections of poetry, two volumes of short stories, and ten works of nonfiction. He has contributed to *The New Yorker, Harvard Review,* the *American Poetry Review,* the *New York Times, Ploughshares,* the *Literary Review,* and dozens of other periodicals. His poetry was selected for inclusion in *The Best American Poetry 2019.* Winner of a National Book Award Bronze Medal, a Fulbright-Hays Exchange Award, the Western States Book Award, a National Council on the Arts Award, the Stephen Henderson Poetry Award for Outstanding Achievement, the Congressional Black Caucus Foundation Award for Lifetime Achievement in the Arts, the PEN Oakland Reginald Lockett Lifetime Achievement Award, and many other awards and grants, Major represented the United States at the International Poetry Festival in Yugoslavia in 1975. In 2021, he was elected to the Georgia Writers Hall of Fame.

Nate Marshall is an award-winning writer, rapper, educator, and editor. He is the author and editor of numerous works, including *Wild Hundreds* and *The BreakBeat Poets: New American Poetry in the Age of Hip-Hop.* Marshall is a member of the Dark Noise Collective and codirects Crescendo Literary. He is an assistant professor of English at Colorado College. He is from the South Side of Chicago.

Dr. Tonya Maria Matthews is a poet, essayist, and creative fiction writer. Her studies in engineering, African American history, and DEI frameworks inspire unique, signature observations in her writing and public speaking. Matthews credits her penchant for empathetic rabble-rousing to her parents, the eighties, a hard-won rite of passage through the southern Ivy League, faith, and a lifelong love affair with Black Joy. The author of *Still Swingin': New and Selected Poems from These Hips,* she is currently the president and CEO of the International African American Museum in Charleston, South Carolina.

Shane McCrae is the author of several books of poetry and the memoir *Pulling the Chariot of the Sun.* His awards include a Lannan Literary Award and a Whiting Award, and he has received fellowships from the Guggenheim Foundation and the National Endowment for the Arts. He lives in New York City and teaches at Columbia University.

Mark McMorris is an award-winning poet born in Kingston, Jamaica, whose books include *Entrepôt* and *The Blaze of the Poui,* a finalist for the Lenore Marshall Poetry Prize. He has been a fellow at the MacDowell Colony, a writer-in-residence at Brown University, and a visiting professor at the University of California, Berkeley. He was recently the director of the Lannan Center for Poetics and Social Practice at Georgetown University, where he currently teaches.

Tony Medina is a multi-genre author and editor of twenty-four award-winning books for adults and young people, the most recent of which are *Che Che Colé* (fiction), *Death, with Occasional Smiling* (poetry), *Thirteen Ways of Looking at a Black Boy* (children's), *I Am Alfonso Jones* (graphic novel), and *Resisting Arrest: Poems to Stretch the Sky* (anthology). The first professor of creative writing at Howard University, Medina holds a master's and PhD from Binghamton University, SUNY. Medina's work appears in more than one hundred anthologies and journals, and his *I and I Bob Marley* audiobook, narrated by actor Jaime Lincoln Smith and produced by Live Oak Media, received the 2022 Audie Award in the Young Listeners category.

E. Ethelbert Miller is a writer and literary activist. He is the author of two memoirs and several books of poetry, including a comprehensive collection that represents more than forty years of his work. Miller served as the editor of *Poet Lore*, the oldest poetry magazine published in the United States. His poetry has been translated into nearly a dozen languages. Miller is a two-time Fulbright Senior Specialist Program Fellow to Israel. He holds an honorary doctor of literature degree from Emory and Henry College and has taught at several universities. He hosts the weekly WPFW morning radio show *On the Margin with E. Ethelbert Miller* and is the host and producer of the series *The Scholars* on the University of the District of Columbia's cable channel. Miller was inducted into the 2015 Washington DC Hall of Fame and awarded the 2016 AWP George Garrett Award for Outstanding Community Service in Literature and the 2016 DC Mayor's Arts Award for Distinguished Honor. He was awarded a 2020 grant by the DC Commission on the Arts and Humanities. Miller's book *If God Invented Baseball,* published by City Point Press, was awarded the 2019 Literary Award for poetry by the Black Caucus of the American Library Association.

Anis Mojgani was born and raised in New Orleans. He is the author of five books of poetry, most recently *In the Pockets of Small Gods* (Write Bloody Publishing, 2018). He also wrote the libretto for the opera *Sanctuaries* (Third Angle Music, 2021), which revolves around the gentrification and displacement of North Portland and the African Diaspora. In 2021, he received an Academy of American Poets Laureate Fellowship while serving as Oregon's tenth poet laureate. He is a two-time National Poetry Slam Individual Champion and a winner of the international World Cup Poetry Slam.

Jessica Care Moore is the author of several poetry collections, including *We Want Our Bodies Back, The Alphabet Verses The Ghetto,* and *The Words Don't Fit in My Mouth.* A Knights Arts grant recipient and the founder of Moore Black Press, she lives in Detroit.

Harryette Mullen's poetry collections include *Open Leaves, Urban Tumbleweed, Recyclopedia,* and *Sleeping with the Dictionary.* Her essays and interviews are collected in *The Cracks Between What We Are and What We Are Supposed to Be.* She teaches literature and creative writing at UCLA.

Yvette R. Murray is an award-winning poet and the author of *Hush, Puppy.* She is the 2022 Susan Laughter Meyers fellow, a 2021 Best New Poet selection, a Watering Hole fellow, and a Pushcart Prize nominee.

Marilyn Nelson is the author or translator of some twenty poetry books and chapbooks for adults, young adults, and children. Many of her collections have won awards, and her poems have been widely anthologized. Nelson's honors include two National Endowment for the Arts creative writing fellowships, the 1990 Connecticut Arts Award, a Fulbright Teaching Fellowship (in the South of France), a Guggenheim Fellowship, the Ruth Lilly Award, the Robert Frost Medal, and the Wallace Stevens Award. She has served as a chancellor of the Academy of American Poets, as poet-in-residence of the Poets Corner at the Cathedral of St. John the Divine, and as the poet laureate of Connecticut. A mother of two and grandmother of two, she now lives quietly, retired from a long career in academia, with her daughter and three cats.

January Gill O'Neil is the author of *Rewilding* (2018), *Misery Islands* (2014), and *Underlife* (2009). She is an assistant professor of English at Salem State University and serves on the board of trustees for the Association of Writers and Writing Programs and Montserrat College of Art. From 2012 to 2018, she served as executive director of the Massachusetts Poetry Festival. She is a Cave Canem fellow, and her poems and articles have appeared in the Academy of American Poets' *Poem-a-Day* series, the *American Poetry Review,* the *New England Review, Ploughshares,* and *Ecotone,* among other publications. She lives with her two children in Beverly, Massachusetts.

Gregory Pardlo is the author of the poetry collections *Spectral Evidence* and *Digest,* winner of the 2015 Pulitzer Prize for Poetry. He is the codirector of the Institute for the Study of Global Racial Justice at Rutgers University–Camden and a visiting professor of creative writing at NYU Abu Dhabi.

Morgan Parker is a poet, essayist, and novelist. She is the author of the young adult novel *Who Put This Song On?* and the poetry collections *Other People's Comfort Keeps Me Up at Night*, *There Are More Beautiful Things Than Beyoncé*, and *Magical Negro*, which won the 2019 National Book Critics Circle Award. Parker's debut book of nonfiction is forthcoming from One World. She is the recipient of a National Endowment for the Arts Literature Fellowship and the winner of a Pushcart Prize, and she has been hailed by the *New York Times* as a "dynamic craftsperson" of "considerable consequence to American poetry."

Willie Perdomo is the author of *Smoking Lovely: The Remix*, *The Crazy Bunch*, *The Essential Hits of Shorty Bon Bon*, and *Where a Nickel Costs a Dime*. Winner of the Foundation for Contemporary Arts Cy Twombly Award for Poetry, the New York City Book Award in Poetry, and the PEN Open Book Award, Perdomo was also a finalist for the National Book Critics Circle Award and the Poetry Society of America Norma Farber First Book Award. He is the coeditor of the anthology *Latínext*, and his work has appeared in the *New York Times Magazine*, *Poetry*, the *Washington Post*, *The Best American Poetry 2019*, and *African Voices*. He is currently a Lucas Arts Literary Fellow, a core faculty member at the Voices of our Nations Writing Workshop, and a teacher at Phillips Exeter Academy.

Xan Forest Phillips is the author of *Hull*, winner of the Lambda Literary Award for Transgender Poetry. They are the winner of a Whiting Award and the Judith A. Markowitz Award for Emerging Writers. A 2019–2020 First Wave Poetry fellow at the Wisconsin Institute for Creative Writing, they live in Chicago.

Kevin Powell is one of the most acclaimed political, cultural, literary, and hip-hop voices in the United States. A poet, journalist, civil and human rights activist, and filmmaker, he is the author of fourteen books, including, most recently, *Grocery Shopping with My Mother*. Powell's next title will be a biography of Tupac Shakur. A native of Jersey City, he lives in Brooklyn.

Joy Priest is the author of *Horsepower*, which won the Donald Hall Prize for Poetry, and the editor of *Once a City Said: A Louisville Poets Anthology*. She has received fellowships from the National Endowment for the Arts and the Fine Arts Work Center. She is currently an assistant professor of African American/African Diaspora poetry in the writing program at the University of Pittsburgh and the curator of community programs and praxis at the Center for African American Poetry and Poetics.

Claudia Rankine is the author of five books of poetry, including *Citizen: An American Lyric* and *Don't Let Me Be Lonely: An American Lyric*, three plays, including *HELP*, which premiered in March 2020 (The Shed, NYC), and *The White Card*, which premiered in February 2018 (Arts-Emerson/American Repertory Theater) and was published by Graywolf Press in 2019, as well as numerous video collaborations. She is also the coeditor of several anthologies, including *The Racial Imaginary: Writers on Race in the Life of the Mind*. Among her numerous awards and honors, Rankine is the recipient of the Bobbitt National Prize for Poetry, the Poets & Writers' Jackson Poetry Prize, and fellowships from the Guggenheim Foundation, the Lannan Foundation, the MacArthur Foundation, United States Artists, and the National Endowment for the Arts. A former chancellor of the Academy of American Poets, she joined the NYU creative writing program in 2021. She lives in New York.

Glenis Redmond is an award-winning performance poet, praise poet, educator, and writer from North Carolina. For the past thirteen years, she has traveled both domestically and abroad, carrying the message of poetry to the masses. She has been published in *Meridians, Heartstone, Black Arts Quarterly, Obsidian II: Black Literature in Review, Emrys Journal, Bum Rush the Page: A Def Poetry Jam,* and *Poetry Slam: The Competitive Art of Performance.* Her work will appear in the upcoming *F Spec* and *Appalachian Heritage* journals. Redmond was a recipient of a Vermont Writing Center Fellowship granted by the William Matthews Estate in 2002. She won the North Carolina Literary Fellowship in 2005.

Justin Phillip Reed is an American poet living in St. Louis. His work appears in the *African American Review, Best American Essays, Callaloo,* the *Kenyon Review, Obsidian,* and elsewhere. He holds a BA in creative writing from Tusculum College and an MFA in poetry from Washington University in St. Louis. The author of the chapbook *A History of Flamboyance,* he has received fellowships from Cave Canem and the Conversation Literary Festival. Reed currently organizes the St. Louis community-based poetry workshop series Most Folks at Work. He was born and raised in South Carolina.

Roger Reeves's poems have appeared in the journals *Poetry, Ploughshares, American Poetry Review, Boston Review,* and *Tin House,* among others. Kim Addonizio selected "Kletic of Walt Whitman" for the Best New Poets 2009 anthology. He has been awarded an NEA Fellowship (2013), a Ruth Lilly Fellowship by the Poetry Foundation (2008), two Bread Loaf Scholarships, an Alberta H. Walker Scholarship from the Provincetown Fine Arts Work Center, and two Cave Canem Fellowships. He earned his PhD at the

University of Texas at Austin and is currently an assistant professor of poetry at the University of Illinois, Chicago. His first book is *King Me*.

Jason Reynolds is a #1 *New York Times* bestselling author of many award-winning books, including *Look Both Ways: A Tale Told in Ten Blocks, All American Boys* (with Brendan Kiely), *Long Way Down, Stamped: Racism, Antiracism, and You* (with Ibram X. Kendi), *Stuntboy, in the Meantime* (illustrated by Raúl the Third), and *Ain't Burned All the Bright* (with artwork by Jason Griffin). The recipient of a Newbery Honor, a Printz Honor, an NAACP Image Award, and multiple Coretta Scott King Honors, Reynolds is also the 2020–2022 National Ambassador for Young People's Literature. He has appeared on *The Late Show with Stephen Colbert, The Daily Show with Trevor Noah, Late Night with Seth Meyers, CBS Sunday Morning, Good Morning America,* and various other media outlets. He is on the faculty of the Writing for Young People MFA program at Lesley University and lives in Washington, DC.

Maritza Rivera is a Puerto Rican poet, Army veteran, and literary translator who resides in Rockville, Maryland, and San Juan, Puerto Rico. She has been writing poetry for more than fifty years and is the creator of a short form of poetry called blackjack. Since 2011, Maritza has hosted the Mariposa Poetry Retreat and the Mariposa Poetry Reunion.

Lucinda Roy, a distinguished professor in creative writing at Virginia Tech, is the author of four novels, three collections of poetry, and a memoir. Her most recent novels are *The Freedom Race* and *Flying the Coop,* volumes 1 and 2 in her futuristic slave narrative trilogy. She is also the author-illustrator of the forthcoming children's book *Sailing Home on an Elephant.*

Kalamu ya Salaam is an American poet, author, filmmaker, and teacher from the Ninth Ward of New Orleans. He was the founder of BLCK-ARTSOUTH, served as an editor for the *Black Collegian* and *QBR: The Black Book Review,* and was also the founder and director of the NOMMO Literary Society, a New Orleans–based Black writers' workshop. The author of several books of poetry, most recently, *Be About the Beauty,* he is a well-known activist and social critic who has spoken out on a number of racial and human rights issues.

Sonia Sanchez—poet, activist, scholar—was the Laura Carnell Professor of English and Women's Studies at Temple University. She is the recipient of both the Robert Frost Medal for "distinguished lifetime service to American poetry" and the Langston Hughes Poetry Award. One of the most important writers of the Black Arts Movement, Sanchez is the author of sixteen books.

Poet and essayist Chet'la Sebree is the author of *Field Study,* winner of the 2020 James Laughlin Award from the Academy of American Poets, and *Mistress.* She teaches at George Washington University.

Tim Seibles is the author of seven collections of poetry, including *Body Moves* (1988), *Hurdy-Gurdy* (1992), *Hammerlock* (1999), *Buffalo Head Solos* (2004), *Fast Animal* (2012), which won the Theodore Roethke Memorial Poetry Prize, received the PEN Oakland/Josephine Miles Literary Award, and was nominated for a 2012 National Book Award, and *One Turn Around The Sun* (2017). His latest book of poetry, *Voodoo Libretto,* was published by Etruscan Press in 2022. His poems have been published in the *Indiana Review, Black Renaissance Noire, Cortland*

Review, Ploughshares, Massachusetts Review, Beloit Poetry Journal, Best American Poetry, and numerous other literary journals and anthologies. Seibles lives in Norfolk, Virginia, where he teaches at Old Dominion University.

Aisha Sharif is a Cave Canem fellow whose poetry has appeared in *Rattle, Callaloo, Crab Orchard Review, Tidal Basin Review,* and *Calyx.* She earned her MFA in creative writing at Indiana University Bloomington and her BA in English from Rhodes College in Memphis.

Warsan Shire is a writer and poet. Her debut pamphlet, *Teaching My Mother How to Give Birth,* was published in 2011 and has gone on to be a bestselling book of poetry. She won the inaugural Brunel University African Poetry Prize in 2013, and in 2014 she was appointed London's first young poet laureate. She was also selected as poet-in-residence for Queensland, Australia, where she collaborated with the Aboriginal Centre for Performing Arts. In 2015, Shire released a limited-edition pamphlet, *Her Blue Body,* and in 2016 did the film adaptation and poetry for the visual album *Lemonade.* In 2017, she was included as part of the Penguin Modern Poets series, alongside Sharon Olds and Malika Booker. Warsan lives in Los Angeles and is working on her first collection.

Evie Shockley, poet and scholar, thinks, creates, and writes with her eye on a Black feminist horizon. Her books of poetry include *suddenly we, semiautomatic,* and *the new black.* Her work, which appears internationally, has twice garnered the Hurston/Wright Legacy Award and was a finalist for the Pulitzer Prize. Her other honors include the Lannan Literary Award for Poetry and the Stephen Henderson Award, and her joys include participating in such communities as Poets at the End of the World, Cave Canem, and the Community of Writers. Shockley is the Zora Neale Hurston Distinguished Professor of English at Rutgers University. Her most recent collection, *Suddenly We,* was short-listed for the National Book Award.

Safiya Sinclair is the author of the memoir *How to Say Babylon* and the poetry collection *Cannibal,* winner of a Whiting Award, the American Academy of Arts and Letters' Metcalf Award, the OCM Bocas Prize for Caribbean Poetry, the Phillis Wheatley Book Award, and the Prairie Schooner Book Prize in Poetry. Her other honors include a Pushcart Prize, fellowships from the Poetry Foundation, MacDowell, Yaddo, and the Bread Loaf Writers' Conference. Her work has appeared in *The New Yorker, Granta, The Nation, Poetry,* the *Kenyon Review,* the *Oxford American,* and elsewhere. She received her MFA in poetry at the University of Virginia and her PhD in literature and creative writing from the University of Southern California. She is currently an associate professor of creative writing at Arizona State University.

Chris Slaughter graduated from Medgar Evers College with a degree in English with a concentration in creative writing. He earned an MFA in poetry from Hunter College, where he received a Shuster Award for his master's thesis. He has also received fellowships from Cave Canem, the North Country Institute and Retreat for Writers of Color, and Brooklyn Poets. Born and raised in Brooklyn, he has dedicated himself to traveling and working on ways of bringing new voices to his writing. Chris works as a director of programs at Eagle Academy for Young Men of Harlem while chipping away at his new manuscript, *Dig.*

Clint Smith is the author of the poetry collections *Above Ground* and *Counting Descent,* as well as a meta-historical travelogue novel *How the Word Is Passed: A Reckoning with the History of Slavery Across America* (2021). *Counting Descent* won the 2017 Literary Award for Best Poetry Book from the Black Caucus of the American Library Association and was a finalist for an NAACP Image Award. Smith has received fellowships from the Andrew W. Mellon Foundation, New America, the Emerson Collective, the Art for Justice Fund, Cave Canem, and the National Science Foundation. He earned his PhD in education from Harvard University and writes for *The Atlantic.* He lives in Maryland with his wife and their two children.

Jasmine Elizabeth Smith is a poet from Oklahoma. She received an MFA from the University of California, Riverside, and she is a Cave Canem and Black Earth Institute fellow. Smith's poetic work is a confluence of poetry of witness, archival research, and radical imagination, in which she constructs the narratives of both real and invented characters as a space where previously conceived notions of the Black experience can be challenged, complicated, and dismantled. Her debut collection, *South Flight,* was a winner of the 2021 Georgia Poetry Prize.

Tracy K. Smith is a Pulitzer Prize–winning poet, memoirist, editor, translator, and opera librettist. She served as the twenty-second poet laureate of the United States from 2017 to 2019, during which time she spearheaded "American Conversations: Celebrating Poems in Rural Communities" with the Library of Congress, launched the American Public Media podcast *The Slowdown,* and edited the anthology *American Journal: Fifty Poems for Our Time.* She is a professor of English and of African and African American Studies at Harvard University.

Bianca Lynne Spriggs is an award-winning writer and multidisciplinary artist from Lexington, Kentucky. An assistant professor of English at Ohio University, Spriggs is the author of four collections of poems, most recently *Call Her By Her Name* and *The Galaxy Is a Dance Floor*. She is the coeditor of three poetry anthologies, most recently *Undead: Ghouls, Ghosts, and More* and *Black Bone: 25 Years of the Affrilachian Poets*.

Lolita Stewart-White is a poet, filmmaker, and educator who lives and works in Miami. Her poems have appeared in the *Iowa Review, Callaloo, Rattle,* and *Beloit Poetry Journal*. She has received fellowships from Cave Canem, South Florida Cultural Consortium, and Sundance Screenwriters Lab. She is a Pushcart Award nominee and the winner of the Paris-American Poetry Prize. Her films have been exhibited at the Museum of Contemporary Art in Miami, the Pan African-American Film and Arts Festival at the Magic Johnson Theater in Los Angeles, and the Seattle Langston Hughes Film Festival.

Sharan Strange grew up in Orangeburg, South Carolina, and was educated at Harvard College. She received her MFA in poetry from Sarah Lawrence College. The author of *Ash,* which won the 2000 Barnard New Women Poets Prize, she is a contributing and advisory editor of *Callaloo* and a co-founder of the Dark Room Collective. Strange has been a writer-in-residence at Fisk University, Spelman College, the University of California, Davis, and the California Institute of the Arts. She teaches at Spelman College.

Pamela L. Taylor lives and works in the Boston area, chronicling her experiences as a poet with a non-literary career. Her work has appeared in the *Adirondack Review, JAMA: Journal of the American Medical*

Association, and *Pedestal Magazine.* She has a doctorate in social psychology from UCLA and an MFA in writing from the Vermont College of Fine Arts, and she is a Cave Canem fellow.

Ronda Taylor is a Creative. She is a poet, writer, and storyteller based in Charleston, South Carolina. She has a passion for writing children's books. She is also the founder and visionary of FLYbara, an organization that equips and empowers a diverse community of Creatives. As a leader, Taylor is motivated to help others reach their full potential. She performs poetry, leads workshops, provides editing services, and speaks at events in her community. While she cocreates with the Creator, her greatest purpose is to make God's unfailing love widely known through the power of words.

Sheree Renée Thomas is an award-winning fiction writer, poet, and editor. Her work is inspired by myth and folklore, natural science, and the genius of the Mississippi Delta. She is a coeditor of *Africa Risen: A New Era of Speculative Fiction* (Tordotcom) and *Trouble the Waters: Tales of the Deep Blue* (Third Man Books). Her fiction collection, *Nine Bar Blues: Stories from an Ancient Future,* was a finalist for the 2021 Ignyte, Locus, and World Fantasy Awards. She is the editor of *The Magazine of Fantasy & Science Fiction,* associate editor of *Obsidian,* and editor of the two-time World Fantasy Award–winning groundbreaking anthologies *Dark Matter: A Century of Speculative Fiction from the African Diaspora* and *Dark Matter: Reading the Bones* (Grand Central). She lives in Memphis near a river and a pyramid.

Truth Thomas is a singer-songwriter and poet who was born in Knoxville, Tennessee, and raised in Washington, DC. He is the author of four collections of poetry: *Speak Water,* winner of a 2013 NAACP Image Award, *Bottle of Life, A Day of Presence,* and *Party of Black.* Thomas's work has twice been nominated for the Pushcart Prize. His poems have appeared in more than seventy publications, including *Callaloo,* the *Newtowner Magazine, New York Quarterly,* the *Emerson Review, The Ringing Ear: Black Poets Lean South* (Cave Canem Anthology), and *The 100 Best African American Poems* (edited by Nikki Giovanni).

Samantha Thornhill is an international literary, spoken word, and teaching artist from Trinidad and Tobago and the United States. After graduating with her MFA in poetry from the University of Virginia, Thornhill taught poetry at the Juilliard School for ten years. The author of almost a dozen children's books, Samantha recently released her debut poetry collection, *The Animated Universe.*

Natasha Trethewey, a Pulitzer Prize–winning poet, served two terms as the nineteenth poet laureate of the United States while also serving as the poet laureate of Mississippi. She is the author of the *New York Times* bestseller *Memorial Drive: A Daughter's Memoir* (2020), a book of nonfiction, *Beyond Katrina: A Meditation on the Mississippi Gulf Coast* (2010), and five collections of poetry. She is the recipient of fellowships from the Academy of American Poets, the National Endowment for the Arts, the Guggenheim Foundation, the Rockefeller Foundation, the Beinecke Library at Yale, and the Radcliffe Institute for Advanced Study at Harvard. From 2015 to 2016, she served as poetry editor of the *New York Times Magazine.* In 2017, she received the Heinz Award for Arts and Humanities, and, in 2020, she received the Rebekah Johnson Bobbitt National Prize for Lifetime Achievement in Poetry from the Library of

Congress. A member of both the American Academy of Arts and Letters and the American Academy of Arts and Sciences, she was elected to the board of chancellors of the Academy of American Poets in 2019. She is also the Board of Trustees Professor of English in the Weinberg College of Arts and Sciences at Northwestern University.

Jacqueline Allen Trimble lives in Montgomery, Alabama. She is a National Endowment for the Arts creative writing fellow, a Cave Canem fellow, and an Alabama State Council on the Arts literary fellow. *American Happiness,* her debut collection, won the Balcones Poetry Prize.

Quincy Troupe is the award-winning author of twenty-one books, including twelve volumes of poetry and three children's books. His writings have been translated into more than thirty languages. Among his many distinguished achievements are the Paterson Award for Sustained Literary Achievement, the Milt Kessler Poetry Book Award, three American Book Awards, the 2014 Gwendolyn Brooks Poetry Award, a 2014 Lifetime Achievement Award from Furious Flower, and the 2018 Charles H. Wright Museum of African American History Award.

Alice Walker is an internationally celebrated writer, poet, and activist whose books include seven novels, four collections of short stories, four children's books, and volumes of essays and poetry. She won the Pulitzer Prize for Fiction and the National Book Award for *The Color Purple* in 1983.

Frank X Walker is the author of *A is for Affrilachia,* among other titles. The recipient of fellowships from the Lannan Foundation, the NAACP, the Black Caucus of the American Library Association, and other organizations, he served as the poet laureate of Kentucky from 2013 to 2014. He lives in Lexington, Kentucky.

Renée Watson is a #1 *New York Times* bestselling author. Her young adult novel *Piecing Me Together* received a Newbery Honor and a Coretta Scott King Award. Her children's picture books and novels for teens have received several awards and international recognition. Her picture books include *A Place Where Hurricanes Happen, Harlem's Little Blackbird: The Story of Florence Mills,* and *The 1619 Project: Born on the Water,* written with Nikole Hannah-Jones. Watson grew up in Oregon and splits her time between Portland and Harlem.

Afaa Michael Weaver, formerly known as Michael S. Weaver, is an American poet, short-story writer, and editor. He is the author of numerous poetry collections, and his honors include a Fulbright Scholarship, fellowships from the National Endowment for the Arts and Pew Foundation, and a Kingsley Tufts Poetry Award. He won the PDI Award in playwriting from the ETA Creative Arts Foundation in Chicago for his play *Elvira and the Lost Prince.* His poetry has been translated into Arabic and Chinese, and, having studied at the Taipei Language Institute in Taiwan, he has translated and written poems of his own in Chinese. Weaver was the first African American poet to serve as poet-in-residence at Bucknell University's Stadler Center, and he has also taught at NYU, City University of New York, Seton Hall Law School, Rutgers University, and the Bread Loaf Writers' Conference. He held an endowed chair at Simmons College for twenty years. He has been on the faculty at Cave Canem since its inception and in 1998 became Cave Canem's first elder.

Afaa and his wife, Kristen, live in a small farmhouse in the Hudson Valley.

Arisa White is an associate professor of English and creative writing at Colby College. She is the author of *Who's Your Daddy,* coeditor of *Home Is Where You Queer Your Heart,* and coauthor of *Biddy Mason Speaks Up,* the second book in the Fighting for Justice series for young readers. She is the librettist for *Post Pardon: The Opera,* composed by Jessica Jones.

Marcus Wicker was born in Ann Arbor and raised in Ypsilanti, Michigan. He is the author of *Silencer,* winner of the Society of Midland Authors Award, and *Maybe the Saddest Thing,* selected by D. A. Powell for the National Poetry Series. A 2023–2024 Harvard Radcliffe Institute fellow, he has received a National Endowment for the Arts Creative Writing Fellowship, the Poetry Society of America's Lyric Poetry Award, a Pushcart Prize, and a Ruth Lilly Fellowship, as well as fellowships from the Fine Arts Work Center in Provincetown and Cave Canem.

L. Lamar Wilson is the author of *Sacrilegion*—the 2012 selection for the Carolina Wren Press Poetry Series, a 2013 Independent Publishers Group bronze medalist, and a 2013 Thom Gunn Award for Gay Poetry finalist—and coauthor of *Prime: Poetry and Conversation* (Sibling Rivalry Press, 2014), with Phillip B. Williams, Rickey Laurentiis, Saeed Jones, and Darrel Alejandro Holnes. *The Changing Same,* a documentary short film based on his Pushcart-nominated poem "Resurrection Sunday," won a special jury prize at the 2018 New Orleans Film Festival. He is an assistant professor of creative writing at Florida State University.

Yolanda Wisher is a Philadelphia-based poet, bandleader, educator, and curator. She is the author of *Monk Eats an Afro* and the coeditor of the anthology *Peace Is a Haiku Song,* with Sonia Sanchez. In 2016, she was named the third poet laureate of Philadelphia. In 2022, she released the spoken-word album *Doublehanded Suite* with her band Yolanda Wisher & The Afroeaters.

Jacqueline Woodson is the *New York Times* bestselling author of more than fifty books for young people and adults, including *Red at the Bone, Brown Girl Dreaming,* and *The Day You Begin.* She is the recipient of a MacArthur Fellowship, a Guggenheim Fellowship, a National Book Award, and the Hans Christian Andersen medal, among other awards.

Kevin Young is the Andrew W. Mellon Director of the Smithsonian's National Museum of African American History and Culture. He previously served as the director of the Schomburg Center for Research in Black Culture. Young is the author of fifteen books of poetry and prose, including *Stones,* short-listed for the T. S. Eliot Prize; *Brown; Blue Laws: Selected and Uncollected Poems, 1995–2015,* long-listed for the National Book Award; *Book of Hours,* winner of the Lenore Marshall Poetry Prize; *Jelly Roll: A Blues,* a finalist for both the National Book Award and the Los Angeles Times Book Prize; *Bunk,* a *New York Times* Notable Book, long-listed for the National Book Award and named on many "Best of" lists for 2017; and *The Grey Album,* winner of the Graywolf Press Nonfiction Prize and the PEN Open Book Award, a *New York Times* Notable Book, and a finalist for the National Book Critics Circle Award for criticism. The poetry editor of *The New Yorker* and host of the magazine's

Poetry Podcast, Young is the editor of nine other volumes, most recently the acclaimed anthology *African American Poetry: 250 Years of Struggle & Song.* He is a member of the American Academy of Arts and Sciences, the American Academy of Arts and Letters, and the Society of American Historians, and he was named a chancellor of the Academy of American Poets in 2020.

ABOUT THE EDITOR

Kwame Alexander is a poet, educator, publisher, two-time Emmy-nominated writer-producer, and #1 *New York Times* bestselling author of thirty-nine books, including *Why Fathers Cry at Night: A Memoir in Love Poems, Recipes, Letters, and Remembrances; The Door of No Return;* and *Light for the World to See: A Thousand Words on Race and Hope.* A regular contributor to NPR's *Morning Edition,* Alexander is the recipient of a Lee Bennett Hopkins Poetry Award, the Coretta Scott King Author Honor Award, three NAACP Image Award nominations, and the 2017 Inaugural Pat Conroy Legacy Award. In 2018, he founded the publishing imprint Versify and opened the Barbara E. Alexander Memorial Library and Health Clinic in Ghana as a part of LEAP for Ghana, an international literacy program he cofounded. You can listen to his podcast, *Why Fathers Cry,* and find him online at KwameAlexander.com.